THE COMPLETE
VEGGIE
AIR FRYER
COOKBOOK

THE COMPLETE VEGGIE AIR FRYER COOKBOOK

75 vegetarian and vegan-friendly recipes perfect for your air fryer

CONTENTS

A SUPER EASY GUIDE TO AIR FRYERS

HOW THEY WORK

Air fryers work by circulating hot air around food to cook it quickly with much less oil than roasting or frying. They use a combination of thermal radiation (from a heating element) and rapid convection from a fan (which circulates the hot air very quickly) to cook food extremely efficiently.

The perforated cooking baskets allow this hot air to come into contact with the food easily, giving results that are much closer to frying than baking. However, air fryers rely on minimal oil to achieve beautifully crisp results—giving you the texture of deep-fried foods without heating a pan of oil. And with much less cleaning up.

THE DIFFERENT TYPES OF AIR FRYERS

Air fryers come in a variety of shapes and sizes to suit all households, whether you want to be able to cook individual portions or large family meals in different compartments. Some sit upright and have a deep pull-out drawer (basket air fryers), while some look like mini ovens with wire shelves inside (oven air fryers).

The type you choose will depend on how much space you have available on your kitchen counter top, how much capacity you will need for your family, and what sort of foods you will be cooking.

The recipes in this book were tested in a basket air fryer with a large single drawer (6-quart capacity). For smaller air fryers, you may need to cook some recipes in batches.

BASKET AIR FRYERS

This style of air fryer is the most compact and therefore takes up the least space on your counter top, which is an important factor to consider if you have limited space in your kitchen. Basket air fryers come in a variety of sizes, ranging from 4 quarts to 8 quarts in capacity. They contain a removable perforated basket to hold the food, which allows the hot air to circulate extremely quickly while letting oil and juices drip out.

Basket air fryers are quick (and therefore cost-effective) to heat and easy to clean, but do have a limited capacity, so you may need to cook some food in batches. The other potential downside is that there is no way to see inside while the food is cooking.

OVEN AIR FRYERS

This version is more like a compact oven in style. It has a clear oven door, which allows you to see the food cooking inside on the wire shelves. Oven air fryers take up more space on the counter top and have a larger capacity, which means you can cook different things at the same time. They often include preset functions, as well as a low-temperature mode (useful for dehydrating) and a defrost mode. These can range in size from 5 quarts to 11 quarts in capacity; if you have a smaller one, you may need to cook some things in batches.

SAFETY

Always refer to the manufacturer's instructions for your air fryer and never leave it unattended while on. Remember, the basket or wire rack will get extremely hot, so take great care when adding and removing items. You will need to clean the air fryer after every use, not only washing the basket thoroughly, but also wiping down the outer pan to remove any grease and trapped food.

VEGGIES

Air fryers and vegetables are a match made in heaven. Any vegetables that you are used to roasting, grilling, or frying are fantastic cooked in an air fryer—not to mention potatoes in all their many forms. Patatas Bravas (see p.51) or a Baked Potato (see p.128) can both be cooked to perfection thanks to the speedy circulation of hot air. For an impressive vegan centerpiece, try a Whole Roasted Cauliflower (see p.81).

FRYING

You cannot use an air fryer in the same way as a pan of hot oil when it comes to wet batters, because this technique simply won't work with this method of cooking. However, coating morsels in flour, egg, and Panko breadcrumbs, such as the Crispy Sesame Tofu Bites (see p.72), Halloumi Fries (see p.52), or Garlic & Herb Mac 'n' Cheese Bites (see p.47), works great in the air fryer to create a crispy fried texture without the added calories of deep-frying in oil.

BAKING

Baking can be tricky to accomplish in an air fryer, so the recipes in this book have all been developed to have the right consistency of batter to ensure successful results. From Breakfast Oat Bars (see p.20) and Peach & Raspberry Muffins (see p.25) to start the day to tasty desserts, such as Lemon Drizzle Cake (see p.166) and Cherry Almond Tart (see p.169), you can get excellent and unexpected results in an air fryer. The main thing to bear in mind is the size of your air fryer: make sure your baking dishes will fit comfortably inside with room for the air to circulate.

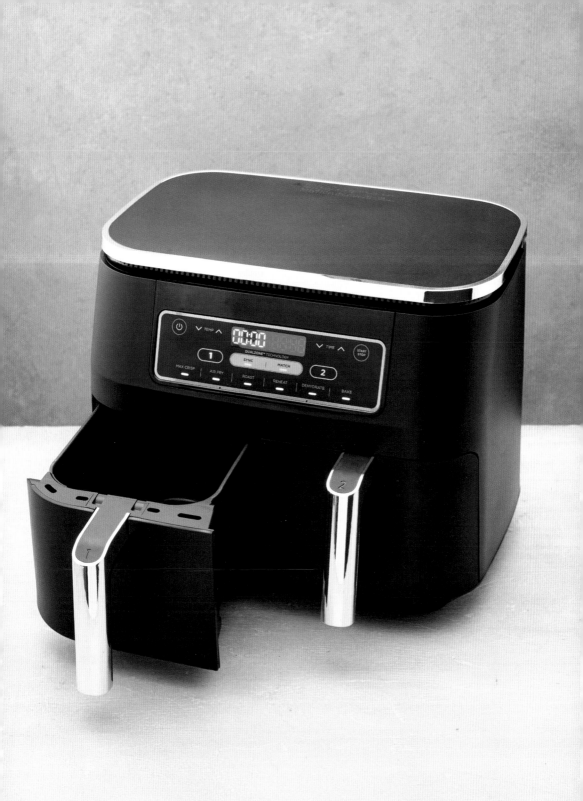

ACCESSORIES

RACKS Most basket-style air fryers come equipped with at least one basic circular rack, while oven air fryers will have wire rack shelves. A toast rack (which sits bread slices upright) is also a useful addition.

PANS When baking in an air fryer, the pan must fit comfortably inside allowing air to circulate all around it, so make sure you have some pans that fit. For baking muffins, you will need a circular tray with muffin inserts. For cakes and tarts, the pan size is given in the recipe, but you may need to adapt this if you have a smaller air fryer.

UTENSILS Invest in tongs, spatulas, and lifters with silicone ends to avoid damaging the protective surface of your air fryer.

SMALL SILICONE MATS You can line the bottom of the air fryer with a silicone mat. Buy them from budget and housewares shops, and simply cut to size to fit your appliance.

SKEWERS These can be useful for making vegetable kebabs or the Tandoori Paneer (see p.106), although you can also use bamboo skewers, soaked well in water first.

5 BEST FOODS TO COOK IN THE AIR FRYER

1 CRISPY POTATOES

2 BREADCRUMB BITES

3 ROASTED VEGGIES

4 PASTRY-WRAPPED PACKAGES

5 CURRIES AND CASSEROLES

BREAKFAST

Whether it's sweet or savory you're after, the air fryer is the perfect tool for whipping up nutritious breakfasts in no time. From fruity muffins to runny baked eggs, ideas range from quick bites to weekend treats.

COCONUT & MAPLE SYRUP ENGLISH MUFFINS (VEGAN)

2 tbsp coconut oil

2 English muffins, split in halves

3½ tbsp maple syrup, plus
    extra to serve

grated zest of 1 orange

¼ cup (60g) coconut yogurt

3 tbsp pistachios, roughly chopped

1 Preheat the air fryer to 350°F/180°C for 3 minutes.

2 Dot the coconut oil evenly on the muffin halves, then drizzle on the maple syrup. Place into the air fryer basket face-side up. Cook at 350°F/180°C for 8 minutes until the muffins are toasted.

3 Meanwhile, stir the grated orange zest into the yogurt.

4 Once cooked, drizzle a little more maple syrup onto the muffins, and sprinkle with the chopped pistachios.

5 Serve with the orange yogurt on the side.

prep + cook time

11 minutes

serves 2

GRANOLA
(VEGAN)

---

2 cups (200g) old fashioned oats

1 cup (150g) mixed nuts, such as almonds, walnuts, and pistachios

2½ tbsp (20g) pumpkin or sunflower seeds

1 tsp ground cinnamon

1 tsp ground ginger

3½ tbsp maple syrup

2 tbsp coconut oil, melted

3 tbsp flaked (slivered) almonds

2½ tbsp (20g) raisins

1 Preheat the air fryer to 285°F/140°C for 3 minutes.
2 In a medium bowl, combine the oats, nuts, seeds, cinnamon, and ginger. Add the maple syrup and coconut oil, and mix well.
3 Add a sheet of foil to the air fryer, and add in the oat mix. Cook at 285°F/140°C for 25 minutes, stirring regularly, until golden.

4 Remove from the air fryer, then add the flaked almonds and raisins.
5 Let cool.

KEEP IT Store in an airtight container for up to 1 month.

prep + cook time
30 minutes
serves 8

RASPBERRY JAM PASTRIES

---

1 sheet premade puff pastry
⅓ cup (130g) raspberry jam
scant ¼ cup (20g) pistachios,
   roughly chopped
1 egg, beaten
powdered sugar, for dusting

1 Preheat the air fryer to 340°F/170°C for 3 minutes.
2 Unroll the pastry and, with the long edge facing you, spread the jam all the way to the edges. Sprinkle on the pistachios, then tightly roll the pastry away from you.
3 Cut the roll into eight pieces. Brush the pastries with the beaten egg.
4 Put the pastries into the air fryer basket flat-side down.

5 Cook at 340°F/170°C for 15 minutes until risen and golden in color.
6 Dust them with powdered sugar and serve.

**prep + cook time
20 minutes
serves 4**

BREAKFAST OAT BARS

6 tbsp (90g) unsalted butter
scant ½ cup (90g) light
   brown sugar
2½ tbsp honey
1¾ cups (175g) old fashioned oats
⅔ cup (80g) blueberries

1 Preheat the air fryer to 340°F/170°C for 3 minutes.
2 Line a 7–in (19-cm) square pan (or one that fits in the air fryer) with parchment paper.
3 In a small saucepan, melt the butter, brown sugar, and honey over low heat.
4 Place the oats in a medium bowl, and pour in the melted butter mixture. Stir well, transfer to the prepared pan, and press the mixture flat.
5 Poke in the blueberries.
6 Bake at 340°F/170°C for 20–25 minutes until golden.
7 Let cool, then cut into bars.

TIP Other berries would work well here; try raspberries or blackberries.

**prep + cook time
30 minutes
serves 4–6**

RHUBARB & GINGER COMPOTE (VEGAN)

11oz (320g) rhubarb, cut into
  1¼-in (3-cm) pieces
2 tbsp (25g) sugar
¾-in (2-cm) piece of ginger,
  peeled and finely grated
juice of ½ lemon
scant 1 cup (200g) coconut yogurt

1 Preheat the air fryer to 325°F/160°C for 3 minutes.
2 Put the rhubarb into a baking dish that fits in the air fryer. Add the sugar, ginger, lemon juice, and a splash of water. Mix well.
3 Cook at 325°F/160°C for 15 minutes until the rhubarb is tender.
4 Divide the yogurt among four bowls, then spoon on the rhubarb.

SERVE IT Serve this with the granola on page 17 sprinkled over the top.

prep + cook time
20 minutes
serves 4

PEACH & RASPBERRY MUFFINS

½ cup (125g) butter, softened

½ cup (110g) sugar

2 eggs

generous ¾ cup (110g) all-purpose flour

1 tsp baking powder

¼ cup (60g) drained canned peaches, cut into ½-in (1-cm) cubes

⅓ cup (40g) raspberries, large ones cut in half, smaller ones left whole

1 Preheat the air fryer to 325°F/160°C for 3 minutes.
2 In a medium bowl, whisk together the butter and sugar with a handheld mixer until light and fluffy.
3 Add the eggs, one at a time, and beat together.
4 Fold in the flour and baking powder, then fold in the peaches and raspberries until everything is incorporated.
5 Divide the mixture among 4–6 silicone muffin molds, then place in the air fryer basket.

6 Cook at 325°F/160°C for 20 minutes until a skewer comes out clean, then let cool.

KEEP IT Store in an airtight container for up to 3 days.

PREP IT The muffins can be made a day in advance.

prep + cook time

25 minutes

serves 4–6

PAN CON TOMATE FLATBREAD (VEGAN)

---

1 cup (130g) all-purpose flour
½ tsp salt
½ tsp baking powder
3 tbsp extra virgin olive oil, plus extra for rolling
2 large ripe tomatoes
1 garlic clove, peeled
2 tbsp pitted Kalamata olives
2 tbsp sun-dried tomatoes
3 sprigs of basil, leaves picked
2 tbsp finely snipped chives

1 In a medium bowl, mix the flour, salt, baking powder, and 1 tablespoon olive oil. Mix, then slowly add about ⅓ cup (80ml) cold water, bit by bit, just until the dough comes together in a shaggy ball. Cover with a damp kitchen towel, and set aside for 20 minutes.

2 Meanwhile, set a strainer over a medium bowl, then grate the tomatoes into it. Season with salt, and leave for a few minutes until the liquid has drained.

3 Add the tomato pulp to another small bowl, then add the remaining olive oil. Mix, and set aside.

4 Preheat the air fryer to 400°F/200°C for 3 minutes.

5 Take the dough out of the bowl, and knead for a minute until smooth.

6 Divide the dough into two balls, then drizzle a little olive oil onto the counter top. Roll each dough ball out into a round disk shape, approximately ½in (1 cm) thick.

7 Put each flatbread into the air fryer basket. Cook at 400°F/200°C for 5 minutes, then turn over and cook for another 3 minutes until golden.

8 Remove the flatbreads from the air fryer, then rub with the peeled garlic clove. Spread the tomato pulp onto the flatbreads. Season with black pepper, and sprinkle with the olives, sun-dried tomatoes, basil leaves, and chives.

**prep + cook time
15 minutes, plus
resting time
serves 2**

CHEESY FRITTATA MUFFINS

½ red onion, thinly sliced
½ red bell pepper, sliced
generous ⅓ cup (50g) frozen peas,
   defrosted
scant ½ cup (50g) grated cheddar
2 tbsp (15g) grated mozzarella
3 eggs
2 English muffins
vegetable or olive oil cooking spray
to serve: arugula and hot sauce
   (optional)

1 Preheat the air fryer to 350°F/180°C for 3 minutes.
2 In a medium bowl, combine the onion, red pepper, peas, cheddar, and mozzarella. Add the eggs, season with salt and black pepper, then mix well to combine.
3 Spray two silicone air fryer ramekins with cooking spray, then divide the mixture between the two ramekins. Cook at 350°F/180°C for 11 minutes.

4 Meanwhile, cut the muffins in half and toast them.
5 Remove the frittatas from the ramekins and place one on the bottom half of each muffin, with a little arugula, if you like.
6 Add a splash of hot sauce, if using, put the muffin tops on, and serve.

**prep + cook time
15 minutes
serves 2**

EGGY BREAD
WITH TOMATOES & HERB OIL

8oz (225g) cherry tomatoes
3 sprigs of thyme, leaves picked
2 tsp sherry vinegar or balsamic
    vinegar
2 eggs
1 tbsp milk
1 tsp dried oregano
2 thick slices of sourdough
¼ cup (15g) finely chopped basil
¼ cup (15g) finely chopped
    flat-leaf parsley
2 sprigs of mint, finely chopped
finely grated zest of 1 lemon
4 tsp extra virgin olive oil
vegetable or olive oil cooking spray

1 Preheat the air fryer to 350°F/180°C for 3 minutes.
2 Add the tomatoes to a baking dish that fits into the air fryer. Sprinkle with the thyme, then add the vinegar. Season with salt and pepper, and cook at 350°F/180°C for 10 minutes.
3 Meanwhile, in a shallow bowl, beat the eggs with the milk and oregano. Season with salt and black pepper, then whisk well. Add the bread and soak for 30 seconds on each side.
4 Line the air fryer basket with foil, add the bread, spray with a little cooking spray, and cook at 350°F/180°C for 5 minutes.

5 Turn the bread over, spray with a little more oil, and cook for a further 3 minutes.
6 Meanwhile, add the basil, parsley, mint, and lemon zest to a small bowl to make the herb oil. Season with a pinch of salt, then add the olive oil. Mix well and set aside.
7 Serve the eggy bread on a plate with the tomatoes, and drizzle with the chopped herbs and oil.

**prep + cook time
20 minutes
serves 2**

31

CHEESY MUSHROOM BAKE

1 tbsp (15g) butter, softened
2 garlic cloves, crushed
4 portobello mushrooms, trimmed
  and stalks removed
2 tbsp extra virgin olive oil
8oz (225g) cherry tomatoes
1 tsp dried oregano
scant ½ cup (50g) grated cheddar
generous ½ cup (70g) grated
  mozzarella
½ cup (25g) basil leaves

1 Preheat the air fryer to 340°F/170°C for 3 minutes.
2 In a small bowl, mix together the butter and crushed garlic.
3 Put the portobello mushrooms into a baking dish that fits in the air fryer. Drizzle with the olive oil, then dot with the garlic butter, and season with salt and black pepper. Cook at 340°F/170°C for 10 minutes.
4 Surround the portobello mushrooms with the cherry tomatoes, and sprinkle with the oregano. Sprinkle both cheeses onto the mushrooms.

5 Increase the heat of the air fryer to 350°F/180°C, and cook for 5 minutes.
6 Once ready, sprinkle with the basil leaves, crack over some black pepper and serve.

**prep + cook time
20 minutes
serves 2**

ASPARAGUS WITH EGGS

& ALMOND DRESSING

½lb (225g) asparagus, trimmed
4 tbsp extra virgin olive oil
4 eggs
⅓ cup (50g) blanched almonds
1 small garlic clove, crushed
2 tsp red wine vinegar
2 tbsp crispy onions

1 Preheat the air fryer to 350°F/180°C for 3 minutes.
2 Add the asparagus to a medium bowl. Drizzle with 1 tablespoon olive oil, then season with salt and black pepper. Put the asparagus and eggs into the air fryer basket, and cook at 350°F/180°C for 7 minutes.
3 Put the remaining olive oil in a blender with ⅓ cup (80ml) water, the almonds, garlic, and vinegar. Season, then blend until smooth.

4 Peel and halve the cooked eggs.
5 Serve the eggs with the asparagus, and spoon on the dressing. Sprinkle the crispy onions on top, and add a grind of black pepper.

TIP Omit the eggs to make this recipe vegan.

prep + cook time
10 minutes
serves 2

BAKED EGGS
WITH KIMCHI & SPRING GREENS

½ onion, finely chopped
2 garlic cloves, crushed
½ cup (120g) kimchi
1 (14.5oz/400g) can diced tomatoes
2½ cups (50g) spring greens, shredded
2 eggs
¼ cup (30g) finely grated cheddar
1 green onion, finely chopped
handful of cilantro, leaves picked

1 Preheat the air fryer to 340°F/170°C for 3 minutes.
2 Put the onion, garlic, kimchi, and diced tomatoes into a baking dish that fits in the air fryer. Season with salt and black pepper, then cook at 340°F/170°C for 5 minutes.
3 Add the spring greens and a splash of water, and mix well. Using the back of a spoon, make two dips in the mixture, and crack the eggs into them. Sprinkle with the cheese and cook at 340°F/170°C for 10 minutes until the eggs are set.

4 Sprinkle with the green onion and cilantro. Finish with a grind of black pepper.

prep + cook time
20 minutes
serves 2

KHACHAPURI

2 cups (50g) spinach
¼ cup (60g) cream cheese
⅔ cup (80g) grated mozzarella
grated zest of 1 lemon
pinch of chili flakes
all-purpose flour, for dusting
8oz (225g) premade pizza dough
3 eggs
2 green onions, finely chopped
1 tsp nigella seeds

1 Put the spinach in a colander set over the sink, and pour boiling water over the spinach until it wilts. Pour over some cold water to cool. Squeeze the spinach to remove the water, then finely chop and set aside.

2 In a medium bowl, combine the cream cheese, mozzarella, lemon zest, and chili flakes. Season with salt and black pepper, then set aside.

3 Preheat the air fryer to 340°F/170°C for 3 minutes.

4 Sprinkle a little flour onto the counter top, divide the pizza dough in half, then roll each portion out into an oval shape. Fold the edges inward to create a thick border, and pinch the two side edges together.

5 Divide the cheese mixture between the two ovals, spreading it right to the thick edges.

6 In a small bowl, crack one egg and beat well. Brush the edges with the egg, then carefully place each piece of dough onto a sheet of foil. Put them into the air fryer and cook at 340°F/170°C for 7 minutes.

7 Using the back of a spoon, press into each khachapuri to create a dip. Crack an egg into each dip and cook at 340°F/170°C for a further 3 minutes until the egg is set.

8 Sprinkle with the green onions and nigella seeds, then serve.

TIP Substitute the mozzarella to use what you have in the fridge; cheddar also works well.

prep + cook time
15 minutes
serves 2

SNACKS AND SIDES

An air fryer allows you to make side
dishes that can take center stage,
such as jazzing up a side of carrots
with walnuts and yogurt, as well as
snacks that will satisfy all the family.
Crispy sesame tofu bites?
Yes, please!

BABA GANOUSH
WITH PITA CHIPS (VEGAN)

3 tbsp extra virgin olive oil,
   plus extra to serve
2 eggplants, cut in half lengthwise
2 pita breads
2 tbsp tahini
1 tsp ground cumin, plus extra
   to serve
1 garlic clove, crushed
juice of 1 lemon

1 Preheat the air fryer to 350°F/180°C for 3 minutes.
2 Drizzle 2 tablespoons olive oil over the eggplant halves, then put them cut-side down into the air fryer basket, and cook at 350°F/180°C for 20 minutes.
3 Remove the eggplants from the air fryer, and set aside to cool for a few minutes.
4 Meanwhile, cut the pita breads into small triangles, and put them into a medium bowl. Drizzle with the remaining olive oil, and season with a little salt. Put them directly into the air fryer basket and cook at 350°F/180°C for 4 minutes until golden and crispy.
5 Scrape the flesh from the eggplants, then put this into a blender. Add the tahini, cumin, garlic and lemon juice. Season with salt and black pepper, and blend until almost smooth, making sure to retain some texture.
6 Serve the baba ganoush in a bowl, sprinkled with extra cumin. Drizzle with a little extra olive oil and serve the pita chips on the side.

**prep + cook time
30 minutes
serves 4**

SWEET POTATO & PEA SAMOSAS (VEGAN)

---

1 lb (450g) sweet potatoes, peeled
    and cut into ¾-in (2-cm) pieces
½ red onion, finely chopped
2 garlic cloves, finely chopped
¾-in (2-cm) piece of ginger,
    peeled and finely grated
1 tbsp Madras curry paste
2 tbsp extra virgin olive oil,
    plus extra for brushing
⅔ cup (80g) frozen peas
⅓ cup (15g) roughly chopped
    cilantro
5oz (135g) phyllo pastry
1 tbsp nigella seeds
to serve: lime wedges and
    mango chutney

1 Preheat the air fryer to 340°F/170°C for 3 minutes.
2 Fill a medium saucepan with water, and bring to a boil. Once boiling, add the sweet potatoes and cook for 10 minutes until softened. Drain the sweet potatoes and set aside.
3 Meanwhile, in a baking dish that fits in the air fryer, combine the red onion, garlic, ginger, and curry paste. Add the olive oil and season with salt and pepper, then cook at 340°F/170°C for 5 minutes.
4 Put the mixture into a blender and pulse a few times until broken down, but not completely smooth. Transfer to a medium bowl, then add the frozen peas and cilantro. Stir through, then set aside and let cool.
5 Take two sheets of phyllo pastry and lay them flat on the counter top, with the shortest side facing you.

6 Brush one of the sheets with oil and lay the other sheet on top of this. Cut the sheet in half horizontally, then cut each half vertically into three sections, so you end up with six strips.
7 Brush each strip with oil. Place 1 tablespoon of the sweet potato mixture in a triangular shape in the top right corner of each strip. Fold the pastry over to keep the triangular shape, and continue folding over until you reach the bottom.
8 Brush each triangle with more oil, and sprinkle with the nigella seeds.
9 Put the samosas into the air fryer basket, and cook at 340°F/170°C for 10 minutes until golden.

SERVE IT Serve the samosas with lime wedges and some mango chutney.

prep + cook time
25 minutes
makes 6

GARLIC & HERB MAC 'N' CHEESE BITES

⅓lb (150g) macaroni
1 (5oz/150g) package soft garlic
   and herb cream cheese
⅔ cup (70g) grated cheddar
½ tsp cayenne pepper
1 tsp smoked paprika
1 tbsp all-purpose flour
1 egg
1¼ cups (50g) panko breadcrumbs
vegetable or olive oil cooking spray
to serve: snipped chives and
   hot sauce

1 Fill a large saucepan with water and bring to a boil. Add the macaroni, and cook for 6 minutes. Drain, then rinse with cold water to cool the pasta.

2 Add the macaroni to a medium bowl, then add the cream cheese, cheddar, cayenne, paprika, and some salt and pepper. Mix together with your hands until well combined.

3 Roll the mixture into 12 balls, put onto a tray, and set aside in the fridge for 10 minutes.

4 Put the flour, egg, and panko into three separate small shallow dishes. Whisk the egg well, and add a pinch of salt to the flour.

5 Preheat the air fryer to 400°F/200°C for 3 minutes.

6 Coat one macaroni ball in the flour, then the egg, and finally the panko. Put back onto the tray. Repeat this process with all of the macaroni balls.

7 Put the macaroni balls into the air fryer basket, spray generously with cooking spray, and cook at 400°F/200°C for 10 minutes until golden.

8 Put on a platter, sprinkle with the chives, and serve with hot sauce on the side.

TIP You can use any soft cheese flavored with garlic and herbs, or use full-fat cream cheese and substitute the cheddar with Gruyère.

**prep + cook time
30 minutes
serves 4–6**

CHEESE & CHILE CORNBREAD

⅔ cup (100g) cornmeal
¾ cup (100g) all-purpose flour
1 tsp baking powder
1 tsp salt
¾ cup (90g) finely grated cheddar
1 red chile, finely chopped
1 green onion, finely chopped
2 eggs
4 tbsp (60g) butter, melted
⅔ cup (150ml) milk
¾ cup (150g) plain yogurt

1 Preheat the air fryer to 340°F/170°C for 3 minutes.
2 In a large bowl, combine the cornmeal, flour, baking powder, salt, ½ cup (60g) of the cheese, the chile, and green onion, mixing well.
3 In a measuring cup, whisk together the eggs, butter, milk, and yogurt.
4 Make a well in the dry ingredients, and pour in the wet ingredients. Mix with a wooden spoon until smooth.
5 Pour the mix into a greased 8 x 5in (20 x 13cm) loaf pan. Press the mixture down evenly into the pan.

6 Top with the remaining grated cheese and cook at 340°F/170°C for 20 minutes until golden and a skewer comes out clean.

**prep + cook time
25 minutes
serves 4–6**

PATATAS BRAVAS
(VEGAN)

1lb (450g) Yukon Gold potatoes, cut
  into 1¼-in (3-cm) pieces
3 tbsp extra virgin olive oil
½ onion, finely chopped
2 garlic cloves, crushed
1 (14.5oz/400g) can diced tomatoes
1 tsp paprika
1 tsp oregano, plus extra to serve
1 tsp sugar
to serve: snipped chives

1 Preheat the air fryer to 400°F/200°C for 3 minutes.
2 Add the potatoes and 2 tablespoons olive oil to a medium bowl and mix well. Put the potatoes into the air fryer basket, and cook at 400°F/200°C for 20 minutes until golden and crispy.
3 Meanwhile, drizzle the remaining olive oil into a medium saucepan. Add the onion and garlic, and cook for 5 minutes over medium heat.
4 Add the tomatoes and paprika, and simmer over medium–high heat for 10–12 minutes until the sauce has reduced.

5 Add the oregano and sugar, and season well with salt and black pepper.
6 Serve the potatoes in a bowl, topped with the tomato sauce and a sprinkle of snipped chives.

SERVE IT Drizzle over some vegan mayonnaise, if you like.

cook + prep time
25 minutes
serves 2

HALLOUMI FRIES

1½ tablespoons all-purpose flour
1 egg
1¼ cups (50g) panko breadcrumbs
1 tsp paprika
8oz (225g) halloumi cheese,
   cut into ¾-in (2-cm) sticks
1 tbsp honey
1 tbsp za'atar
vegetable or olive oil cooking spray
to serve (optional): chili jam

1 Preheat the air fryer to 400°F/200°C for 3 minutes.
2 Put the flour, egg and panko into three separate small shallow dishes. Whisk the egg well, add a pinch of salt to the flour, and add the paprika to the panko.
3 Coat a halloumi stick in the flour, then the egg, then the panko. Put on a tray, and repeat this process with the rest of the halloumi.

4 Put the cheese into the air fryer basket, and spray generously with cooking spray. Cook at 400°F/200°C for 5 minutes until crisp and golden.
5 Arrange on a platter, then drizzle with the honey and sprinkle with the za'atar. Serve with chili jam, if you like.

prep + cook time
10 minutes
serves 2

SPINACH & FETA BITES

½ onion, finely chopped
2 garlic cloves, crushed
1 tbsp extra virgin olive oil
1 (14oz/400g) package frozen
    spinach, thawed and roughly
    chopped
3 sprigs of mint, roughly chopped
3 sprigs of dill, roughly chopped
scant ¼ cup (45g) cream cheese
¾ cup (100g) crumbled feta
grated zest of 1 lemon
1 premade sheet of puff pastry
1 egg, beaten
1 tsp white sesame seeds
1 tsp black sesame seeds

1 Preheat the air fryer to 285°F/140°C for 3 minutes.
2 Add the onion, garlic and olive oil to a baking dish that fits in the air fryer. Cook at 285°F/140°C for 5 minutes, then let cool.
3 Squeeze the thawed spinach to remove the water. In a medium bowl, combine the spinach, mint, dill, cream cheese, feta, lemon zest, and the cooked onion and garlic. Season with salt and black pepper, mix well, and set aside.
4 Preheat the air fryer to 350°F/180°C for 3 minutes. Unroll the pastry with the longest edge facing you, then cut in half horizontally creating two equal-size strips.
5 Divide the spinach mixture between the two strips, placing it along the center of the strips in a tube shape, leaving a border on the top, bottom and sides.
6 Brush a little egg over the top edge and sides of each strip. Fold over each long edge to meet the other, and press the sides closed. Crimp the edges lightly with a fork.
7 Cut each strip into eight equal pieces, brush the egg over the top of the pastry, and sprinkle with the sesame seeds.
8 Put the bites into the air fryer basket, and cook at 350°F/180°C for 15 minutes until the pastry is crisp and golden.

prep + cook time
25 minutes
serves 4–6

NACHOS
WITH ROASTED CORN CHEESE DIP

½ red onion, thinly sliced

juice of 1 lime

⅓ cup (100g) frozen corn

⅔ cup (80g) grated mozzarella

⅓ cup (40g) grated cheddar

¼ cup (50g) plain yogurt

3 tbsp (40g) mayonnaise

1oz (25g) jarred jalapeños, roughly chopped

3½oz (100g) tortilla chips

to serve: pinch of paprika

1 Preheat the air fryer to 410°F/210°C for 3 minutes.

2 Put the red onion in a small bowl, then add the lime juice and a pinch of salt. Mix and set aside to pickle.

3 Place a piece of foil into the air fryer, then add the corn. Cook at 410°F/210°C for 12 minutes until the corn is roasted.

4 Meanwhile, in a medium bowl, add the mozzarella, cheddar, yogurt, mayonnaise, jalapeños, and a pinch of salt.

5 Add the roasted corn to the cheese bowl and mix well.

6 Add a clean piece of foil to the air fryer and spread the tortilla chips out onto it. Pour the corn mix over the nachos, lower the heat of the air fryer, and cook at 375°F/190°C for 5 minutes.

7 Carefully lift out the foil onto a platter and top with the pickled red onion. Sprinkle with some paprika to serve.

**cook + prep time
20 minutes
serves 4**

NAPA CABBAGE PAKORAS
(VEGAN)

½ head Napa cabbage, shredded
1 carrot, grated
1 onion, finely sliced
¾-in (2-cm) piece of ginger,
    finely grated
1 garlic clove, crushed
¼ tsp ground turmeric
1 tsp garam masala
½ tsp chili powder
1 green chile, seeded and
    finely chopped
2 tbsp cilantro, leaves roughly
    chopped and stalks finely chopped
2 tbsp chickpea (besan) flour
vegetable or olive oil cooking spray
to serve: lime wedges and mango
    chutney (optional)

1 Preheat the air fryer to 375°F/190°C for 3 minutes.
2 In a medium bowl, combine the cabbage, carrot, onion, ginger, garlic, turmeric, garam masala, chili powder, green chile, cilantro leaves and stalks, and a pinch of salt, mixing well.
3 Add the chickpea flour and mix well until combined. Add 2–3 tablespoons of water, a little at a time, adding just enough so the mixture clings together, but it is not overly wet.
4 Take some of the mixture in your hands and shape into a loose ball. Put into the air fryer basket, then repeat with the rest of the mixture.

5 Spray the pakoras generously with cooking spray, and cook at 375°F/190°C for 5 minutes.
6 Spray with more cooking spray, and cook for a further 5 minutes until golden.
7 Serve with lime wedges and mango chutney on the side, if you like.

**prep + cook time
20 minutes
makes 8**

FETA, SPINACH & SUN-DRIED TOMATO SANDWICH

2½ cups (80g) spinach

½ cup (50g) sun-dried tomatoes, roughly chopped, plus a little of the oil from the jar

4 thick slices of bread

¾ cup (100g) thinly sliced feta

2 tbsp (15g) pitted black Kalamata olives

1 green onion, finely sliced

2 tsp capers

1 Put the spinach in a colander over the sink, and pour boiling water over the spinach until it wilts. Rinse with cold water to cool. Squeeze the spinach to remove the water, then finely chop and set aside.

2 Preheat the air fryer to 375°F/190°C for 3 minutes.

3 Brush some oil from the sun-dried tomatoes over one side of each bread slice.

4 Turn two of the slices over and layer them with the feta, spinach, sun-dried tomatoes, olives, green onion, and capers. Put the remaining bread slices on top, oil-side up.

5 Put into the air fryer and cook at 375°F/190°C for 10 minutes until toasted.

prep + cook time
15 minutes
serves 2

PERFECT ROAST POTATOES

1lb (450g) Russet potatoes, cut into
   2½-in (6-cm) pieces
1 tbsp finely chopped rosemary
2 garlic cloves, unpeeled, smashed
2 tbsp extra virgin olive oil
1 tbsp oregano

1 Preheat the air fryer to 400°F/200°C for 3 minutes.
2 In a medium bowl, combine the potatoes, rosemary, garlic, and oil. Season with salt and black pepper.
3 Put into the air fryer basket and cook at 400°F/200°C for 20 minutes, giving them a shake halfway through.

4 Sprinkle with the oregano and serve.

**prep + cook time
25 minutes
serves 4**

HONEYED CARROTS
WITH WALNUTS & YOGURT

⅓ cup (50g) walnut halves
1lb (450g) carrots, peeled, and large ones cut in half, smaller ones left whole
3 tbsp (40g) butter, cut into cubes
2 tbsp extra virgin olive oil
¾ cup (150g) Greek yogurt
grated zest of 1 lemon
2 tbsp honey
2 tbsp pomegranate seeds
2 sprigs of cilantro, leaves picked
2 sprigs of flat-leaf parsley, leaves picked

1 Preheat the air fryer to 340°F/170°C for 3 minutes.
2 Put the walnuts into the air fryer and cook for 4 minutes at 340°F/170°C until golden. Take out, roughly chop, and set aside.
3 Put the carrots in a baking dish that fits into the air fryer, dot with the butter, and drizzle with 1 tablespoon olive oil. Season with salt and pepper, then cook at 340°F/170°C for 15 minutes.
4 Meanwhile, in a small bowl, combine the Greek yogurt, remaining olive oil, and the lemon zest. Season with a little salt, mix well, and set aside.

5 After the 15 minutes, drizzle the honey over the carrots, increase the heat of the air fryer, and cook at 350°F/180°C for 5 minutes.
6 To serve, spread the yogurt out onto a platter, top with the carrots, walnuts, pomegranate seeds, cilantro, and parsley.

**prep + cook time
20 minutes
serves 2**

ROASTED CORN SALAD

½ red onion, thinly sliced
juice of 2 limes, grated zest of 1
1 large flour tortilla, cut into
    ¾-in (2-cm) pieces
2 tbsp (25g) butter, softened
2 tsp chipotle paste
1 tsp oregano
½ tsp smoked paprika
2 ears of fresh corn, shucked and
    silk removed
¾ cup (150g) plain yogurt
2 heads butter lettuce, leaves torn
1 avocado, peeled, pitted, and
    roughly chopped
3½oz (100g) cherry tomatoes,
    halved
½ (14oz/400g) can black beans,
    drained and rinsed
vegetable or olive oil cooking spray

1 In a small bowl, combine the onion and juice of 1 lime. Add a pinch of salt, mix, and set aside to pickle.
2 Preheat the air fryer to 350°F/180°C for 3 minutes.
3 Put the tortilla pieces into the air fryer, spray with cooking spray, then cook at 350°F/180°C for 4 minutes until golden and crispy. Set aside.
4 Meanwhile, put the butter in a small bowl, add 1 teaspoon chipotle paste, the oregano, paprika, and lime zest, then mix well and set aside.
5 Put the corn in the air fryer, spray with cooking spray, increase the heat of the air fryer to 400°F/200°C, and cook for 10 minutes.
6 Turn the corn over, dot with the butter mixture, and cook for 5 minutes more at 400°F/200°C until softened and roasted.
7 In a small bowl, mix the remaining chipotle paste with the yogurt and the juice of 1 lime. Season with salt and pepper, and set aside.
8 To assemble, in a large serving bowl, add the lettuce, avocado, tomatoes, black beans, and tortilla chips. Cut the corn off the cob, and add to the salad. Drizzle with the yogurt dressing and top with the pickled red onion.

**prep + cook time
25 minutes
serves 4**

67

SWEET POTATO PATTIES
(VEGAN)

¾lb (320g) sweet potatoes, peeled and cut into 1½-in (4-cm) cubes
1 green onion, finely sliced
1 tsp smoked paprika
1 tsp ground coriander
2 cups (100g) fresh breadcrumbs
3 tbsp all-purpose flour
½ cup (100g) dairy-free yogurt
3 tbsp cilantro
vegetable or olive oil cooking spray
to serve: snipped chives

1 Fill a large saucepan with water and bring to a boil. Once boiling, add the sweet potatoes and cook for 8 minutes until softened. Drain, then add to a medium bowl and set aside to cool.
2 Preheat the air fryer to 350°F/180°C for 3 minutes.
3 With a fork, mash the sweet potatoes, then add the green onion, paprika, coriander, breadcrumbs, and flour. Season with salt and black pepper, then mix well and shape into six patties.
4 Put into the air fryer basket, spray with cooking spray, and cook at 350°F/180°C for 10 minutes.

5 Turn them over, spray with a little more cooking spray, and cook for a further 5 minutes until cooked through and golden.
6 Put the yogurt and cilantro in a blender and blend until smooth.
7 Serve the patties with the yogurt and sprinkle with some chives.

**prep + cook time
30 minutes
serves 2**

SHISHITO PEPPERS
WITH AIOLI

1lb (450g) shishito or other mild
   peppers, like jalapeño or padrón
6 tbsp (80g) mayonnaise
1 garlic clove, crushed
juice of ½ lemon
1 tbsp finely chopped cilantro
vegetable or olive oil cooking spray

1 Preheat the air fryer to
400°F/200°C for 3 minutes.
2 Add the peppers to the
air fryer, spray with
cooking spray, and cook
at 400°F/200°C for
5 minutes until charred
and slightly softened.
3 Meanwhile, in a small
bowl, combine the
mayonnaise, garlic, lemon
juice, and cilantro. Season
with salt and black pepper,
then mix and set aside.

4 Serve the peppers with
the aioli on the side.

prep + cook time
10 minutes
serves 2

CRISPY SESAME TOFU BITES (VEGAN)

10oz (280g) extra firm tofu, patted
   dry and cut into 12 sticks
3 tbsp soy sauce
3 tbsp cornstarch
2 tbsp plant-based milk
¾ cup (30g) panko breadcrumbs
1 tbsp mix of white and black
   sesame seeds
vegetable or olive oil cooking spray
to serve: sweet chili sauce

1 Put the tofu into a baking dish, add the soy sauce, and marinate for 10 minutes.
2 Preheat the air fryer to 375°F/190°C for 3 minutes.
3 Put the cornstarch, milk, and panko into three separate shallow dishes. Add the sesame seeds to the panko dish and mix well.
4 Coat a piece of tofu first in the cornstarch, then the milk, and then the panko. Place on a baking sheet and repeat with the remaining tofu.

5 Once finished, put all of the tofu in the air fryer basket, spray with cooking spray, and cook at 375°F/190°C for 15 minutes until crispy.
6 Take the tofu pieces out, and serve with sweet chili sauce.

**prep + cook time
30 minutes
serves 2**

KIMCHI & GREEN ONION PANCAKE

2 eggs
2 tbsp soy sauce, plus extra to serve
⅔ cup (160g) kimchi, roughly
    chopped, plus 2 tbsp kimchi brine
1¼ cups (160g) all-purpose flour
2 green onions, finely chopped,
    plus extra to serve
vegetable or olive oil cooking spray

1 Preheat the air fryer to 400°F/200°C for 3 minutes.
2 Crack the eggs into a medium bowl, add the soy sauce, 3½ tablespoons water, and the kimchi brine, and whisk well. Add the flour, and whisk again until the batter is smooth. Fold in the kimchi and green onions.
3 Carefully place a sheet of parchment paper in the air fryer basket and spray with cooking spray.

4 Ladle the mixture onto the parchment paper, creating six pancakes. This may have to be done in batches.
5 Cook the pancakes at 400°F/200°C for 5 minutes until cooked through.
6 Serve sprinkled with extra green onions and soy sauce for dipping.

**prep + cook time
10 minutes
serves 2**

ENTREES

When you need to get a meal on the table in a hurry, the speed of an air fryer is your friend. You can ensure perfectly cooked vegetables thanks to the quick circulation of hot air, meaning vegetarian meals have never been so easy to prepare.

RED PEPPER SOUP
(VEGAN)

2 slices of bread, cut into
½-in (1-cm) pieces
4 garlic cloves, unpeeled and
smashed
3 tbsp extra virgin olive oil
3 red bell peppers, seeded and
roughly chopped
1 red onion, roughly chopped
3 tomatoes, roughly chopped
1 tsp smoked paprika
3 sprigs of thyme
1 tbsp red wine vinegar
to serve: basil leaves

1 Preheat the air fryer to 350°F/180°C for 3 minutes.
2 Add the bread and garlic to a medium bowl. Add 1 tablespoon olive oil and a pinch of salt, and mix well.
3 Put into the air fryer and cook at 350°F/180°C for 5 minutes until golden and crispy, then remove from the air fryer, discard the garlic and set aside.
4 Put the red peppers, red onion, tomatoes, paprika, and thyme sprigs into a baking dish that fits in the air fryer. Drizzle with the remaining olive oil, then season with salt and pepper. Mix well, and cook at 350°F/180°C for 15 minutes until the veggies have softened.

5 Put the veggies into a blender with the red wine vinegar and ⅓ cup (100ml) water, and blend until smooth.
6 Divide the soup between two bowls, top with the croutons and some black pepper, then add some basil leaves and serve.

**prep + cook time
25 minutes
serves 2**

WHOLE ROASTED CAULIFLOWER
(VEGAN)

1 head (2lb/900g) cauliflower, leaves
   trimmed

2 tbsp harissa paste

2 tsp ground coriander

3½ tbsp extra virgin olive oil

1 tbsp pine nuts

2 tbsp tahini

juice of 1 lemon

¾ cup (150g) dairy-free yogurt

1 garlic clove, crushed

2 tbsp roughly chopped
   flat-leaf parsley

1 sprig of mint, leaves picked

2 tbsp pomegranate seeds

1 red chile, thinly sliced

1 Fill a large saucepan with water, and bring to a boil. Once boiling, add the whole cauliflower and cook for 5 minutes. Strain in a colander and set aside to cool.

2 Preheat the air fryer to 375°F/190°C for 3 minutes.

3 Meanwhile, in a small bowl, combine the harissa paste, ground coriander, and olive oil. Mix well then spread the mixture over the cauliflower. Season with salt and pepper, then put into the air fryer basket and cook at 375°F/190°C for about 20 minutes until tender.

4 In a dry skillet, toast the pine nuts until golden, being careful not to burn them. Set aside.

5 In a small bowl, combine the tahini, lemon juice, yogurt, and garlic. Season with salt and pepper, and mix well.

6 Spread the yogurt onto a platter, top with the cauliflower, then sprinkle with the parsley, mint, pomegranate seeds, pine nuts, and red chile.

prep + cook time
30 minutes
serves 2

STUFFED ZUCCHINI
(VEGAN)

3 large zucchini
1 onion, finely chopped
2 garlic cloves, crushed
2 tbsp extra virgin olive oil
1 (9oz/250g) pouch microwavable
   basmati rice
2 tomatoes, seeded and
   finely chopped
3 tbsp roughly chopped
   flat-leaf parsley
2 sprigs of dill, roughly chopped
3 tbsp roughly chopped cilantro
2 tbsp fresh breadcrumbs
grated zest of 1 lemon

1 Preheat the air fryer to 300°F/150°C for 3 minutes.
2 Cut the zucchini in half lengthwise, scoop out the flesh, then roughly chop. Put the flesh in a medium bowl, and place the zucchini on a tray. Set both aside.
3 Put the chopped onion and garlic into a baking dish that fits in the air fryer. Drizzle with 1 tablespoon olive oil, season with salt and pepper, then mix together well. Cook at 300°F/150°C for about 5 minutes until softened.
4 Meanwhile, microwave the basmati rice for 2 minutes according to the pouch instructions.
5 Preheat the air fryer to 340°F/170°C for 3 minutes. Add the rice to the chopped zucchini. Add the tomatoes, parsley, dill and cilantro.
6 Add the softened onion and garlic to the bowl, season with salt and pepper, and mix well.
7 Stuff the zucchini with the rice mixture and top with the breadcrumbs. Drizzle with the remaining oil and cook at 340°F/170°C for 15 minutes until the breadcrumbs are golden and the zucchini is tender.
8 Top with the grated lemon zest and serve.

prep + cook time
25 minutes
serves 3

EGGPLANT KATSU CURRY (VEGAN)

½ cucumber, peeled into
  thin ribbons
2 tsp rice wine vinegar
½ tsp sugar
6 tbsp (50g) all-purpose flour
2¼ cups (100g) panko breadcrumbs
2 eggplants (1½lb/700g), cut into
  ½-in (1-cm) disks
1¼ cups (50g) katsu curry sauce
2 (9oz/250g) pouches microwavable
  basmati rice
vegetable or olive oil cooking spray
to serve: cilantro

1 Put the cucumber ribbons into a small bowl, then add the vinegar, sugar, and a pinch of salt. Set aside.
2 Preheat the air fryer to 350°F/180°C for 3 minutes.
3 Put the flour and panko into two separate shallow bowls. Add 3½ tablespoons water to the flour and mix until smooth.
4 Add one eggplant slice to the flour paste to coat, and then transfer it to the panko to coat both sides. Place it on a tray and repeat with the remaining eggplant slices.
5 Put the eggplant slices into the air fryer, spray with cooking spray and cook at 350°F/180°C for 10 minutes.

6 Flip the eggplant slices over, spray with more cooking spray and cook at 350°F/180°C for a further 10 minutes until golden and crispy.
7 Meanwhile, heat the katsu sauce in a small sauce pan or in a bowl in the microwave.
8 Microwave the rice for 2 minutes according to the pouch instructions, then serve alongside the eggplant slices. Spoon on the sauce and serve with the cucumber and some cilantro to garnish.

**prep + cook time
30 minutes
serves 2**

BUTTERNUT SQUASH GNOCCHI

½ butternut squash, peeled and
   cut into 1¼-in (3-cm) cubes
½ red chile, seeded and
   roughly chopped
3 tbsp extra virgin olive oil
10oz (300g) fresh gnocchi
1 tsp red wine vinegar
2 sprigs of sage, leaves picked
1¾oz (50g) soft blue cheese
2 tbsp finely grated Parmesan

1 Preheat the air fryer to 350°F/180°C for 3 minutes.
2 Put the butternut squash into a baking dish that fits in the air fryer. Add the red chile and 1 tablespoon olive oil, and season with salt and black pepper. Cook at 350°F/180°C for 20 minutes until the butternut squash is tender, then remove and set aside.
3 Put the gnocchi into the air fryer with 1 tablespoon oil and cook at 400°F/200°C for 10 minutes until golden and crispy.
4 Meanwhile, add the butternut squash and chile to a blender with 1¼ cups (300ml) water and blend until smooth. Add the red wine vinegar, then season with salt and black pepper.

5 Add the butternut squash sauce to a medium saucepan and keep warm on low heat until the gnocchi are ready.
6 In a small skillet, heat the remaining oil. Once hot, add the sage leaves and cook until crispy. Remove and set aside.
7 Add the gnocchi to the butternut squash sauce, mix well and then serve. Dot with the blue cheese, sprinkle with the Parmesan and sage.

TIP The sauce can be made a day in advance; simply add a splash of water and reheat.

**prep + cook time
35 minutes
serves 2**

GREEN BEANS
WITH HALLOUMI

½ onion, sliced

4 garlic cloves, thinly sliced

2½ tbsp extra virgin olive oil

½lb (225g) green beans, trimmed
   and halved

4 tomatoes, roughly chopped

1 (14.5oz/400g) can diced tomatoes

¾ cup (80g) pitted green olives

1 cup (200g) couscous

juice of ½ lemon, plus lemon
   wedges to serve

½ cup (15g) roughly chopped
   flat-leaf parsley

3 sprigs of mint, roughly chopped

1¾oz (50g) halloumi cheese, grated

1 Preheat the air fryer to 300°F/150°C for 3 minutes.
2 Add the sliced onion and garlic to a baking dish that fits in the air fryer, then drizzle with the olive oil. Cook at 300°F/150°C for 5 minutes.
3 Add the green beans, both kinds of tomatoes, and olives to the onion and garlic. Cook at 350°F/180°C for about 25 minutes until the green beans are tender.
4 Meanwhile, cook the couscous according to the package instructions.
5 To the green beans, add the lemon juice, parsley and mint. Season with salt and black pepper, and give it a good stir.
6 Top the green beans with the grated halloumi. Serve with the couscous and lemon wedges on the side.

TIP Substitute the halloumi for crumbled feta, or leave the cheese out completely to make it vegan.

prep + cook time
35 minutes
serves 2

SATAY TOFU
(VEGAN)

⅓ cup (70g) smooth peanut butter
scant 1 cup (200ml) coconut milk
2 tbsp soy sauce
1 tbsp vegan fish sauce
½ tsp chili flakes
½ tsp sugar
1 tsp curry powder
1 lb (450g) firm tofu, patted dry and
    cut into 1½-in (4-cm) chunks
2 tbsp cilantro leaves
1 red chile, finely sliced
2 tbsp roasted peanuts,
    roughly chopped
to serve: basmati rice, broccolini,
    and lime wedges

1 In a medium bowl, combine the peanut butter, coconut milk, soy sauce, fish sauce, chili flakes, sugar, and curry powder. Whisk well until smooth.
2 Add the tofu to the marinade and leave to marinate for 20 minutes.
3 Preheat the air fryer at 400°F/200°C for 3 minutes.
4 Place a sheet of foil inside the air fryer basket. Take the tofu out of the marinade (reserving the marinade) and place in the basket. Cook at 400°F/200°C for 10 minutes until golden.
5 To serve, drizzle with the reserved marinade and sprinkle the cilantro, sliced red chile, and chopped roasted peanuts on top.
6 Serve with basmati rice, broccolini, and lime wedges for squeezing.

**prep + cook time
15 minutes, plus
marinating time
serves 4**

VEGGIE SAUSAGE BAKE (VEGAN)

8 vegan sausages

1 red onion, cut into wedges

3 garlic cloves, unpeeled and smashed

2 red bell peppers, roughly chopped

1 (15oz/425g) can lima beans, drained and rinsed

2 sprigs of rosemary

3½ tbsp extra virgin olive oil

½ cup (15g) roughly chopped flat-leaf parsley

3 sprigs of basil, leaves picked

2 tsp capers

1 tsp Dijon mustard

5 cornichons

1 tsp red wine vinegar

1 Preheat the air fryer to 340°F/170°C for 3 minutes.

2 Put the sausages, onion, garlic, red peppers, lima beans, and rosemary sprigs in a baking dish that fits in the air fryer, then drizzle with 1 tablespoon olive oil. Season with salt and black pepper and add a splash of water.

3 Cook at 340°F/170°C for 20 minutes until the vegetables are tender and the sausages are cooked through.

4 Meanwhile, to a blender, add the parsley, basil, capers, Dijon mustard, cornichons, red wine vinegar, and the remaining olive oil. Pulse until smooth to make an herby dressing.

5 Serve the sausage bake with the dressing spooned on top.

prep + cook time
25 minutes
serves 4

CAESAR SALAD

1 (15oz/425g) can chickpeas,
  drained and rinsed
3 tbsp extra virgin olive oil
3½oz (100g) ciabatta, cut into
  1¼-in (3-cm) pieces
½lb (225g) broccolini
4 eggs
¾ cup (150g) Greek yogurt
1 tsp Dijon mustard
1 garlic clove, crushed
2 tsp white wine vinegar
¼ cup (20g) finely grated Parmesan
2 romaine lettuces, roughly chopped
¼ cup (20g) sun-dried tomatoes,
  roughly chopped

1 Preheat the air fryer to 400°F/200°C for 3 minutes.
2 Lay the chickpeas out on a tray and dry with paper towels. Put into a medium bowl and drizzle with 1 tablespoon oil. Put into the air fryer, and cook at 400°F/200°C for 15–20 minutes until crispy, then set aside.
3 Add the ciabatta and broccolini to the bowl, then add 1 tablespoon olive oil. Season with salt and freshly ground pepper. Put into the air fryer basket, along with the eggs, and cook at 350°F/180°C for 7 minutes until the ciabatta croutons are crispy and golden, and the broccolini has softened.

4 Meanwhile, to a blender, add the Greek yogurt, mustard, garlic, vinegar, and three-quarters of the Parmesan, then blend.
5 Peel and halve the eggs. Put the romaine lettuce on a platter, and add the chickpeas, croutons, broccolini, halved eggs, and sun-dried tomatoes.
6 Drizzle with the dressing, sprinkle with the remaining Parmesan, and season with black pepper.

prep + cook time
30 minutes
serves 2

TOFU LARB
(VEGAN)

10oz (280g) firm tofu, patted
   dry and finely chopped
1 tbsp extra virgin olive oil
1 shallot, finely sliced
2 tbsp soy sauce
2 tbsp vegan fish sauce
juice of 1 lime, plus 1 lime,
   cut into wedges
1 tsp chili powder
1 (9oz/250g) pouch microwavable
   basmati rice
2 heads butter lettuce, leaves
   separated
1 red chile, finely sliced
1 carrot, cut into matchsticks
½ cucumber, cut into matchsticks
⅓ cup (50g) roasted peanuts,
   roughly chopped
¾ cup (15g) mint, leaves picked
3 tbsp cilantro leaves

1 Preheat the air fryer to
400°F/200°C for 3 minutes.
2 Put the tofu in a baking
dish that fits in the air
fryer, drizzle with the oil
and cook at 400°F/200°C
for 10 minutes.
3 Put the tofu into a
medium bowl and add the
shallot, soy sauce, and fish
sauce. Mix and set aside
for 10 minutes.
4 Add the lime juice and
chili powder and mix.
5 Meanwhile, microwave
the basmati rice for
2 minutes according to the
pouch instructions.

6 Arrange the cooked rice,
lettuce leaves, tofu, chile,
carrot, cucumber, peanuts,
mint, cilantro, and lime
wedges on a platter,
then serve.

SERVE IT Diners can
fill the lettuce leaves
with the tofu and their
choice of veggies,
herbs, and peanuts.

prep + cook time
25 minutes
serves 2

BAKED FETA PASTA

10oz (300g) penne pasta
1 (8oz/225g) block of feta
8oz (225g) cherry tomatoes
1 shallot, finely chopped
3 garlic cloves, finely sliced
pinch of chili flakes
2 sprigs of thyme, leaves picked
scant ½ cup (40g) pitted green
   olives, roughly chopped
1 tbsp capers
2 tbsp extra virgin olive oil
grated zest of 1 lemon
⅓ cup (15g) basil, leaves picked

1 Preheat the air fryer to 340°F/170°C for 3 minutes.
2 Fill a large saucepan with water and bring to a boil. Once boiling, add a large pinch of salt. Add the pasta, and cook according to package instructions. Reserve a cup of pasta water, then strain.

3 Meanwhile, in a baking dish that fits in the air fryer, add the feta, cherry tomatoes, shallot, garlic, chili flakes, thyme, olives, and capers. Drizzle with the olive oil and season with salt and pepper.

4 Cook at 340°F/170°C for 20 minutes until the feta is soft and the tomatoes are bursting.
5 Add the pasta to the feta, pour some of the pasta water over and mix together. Top with the lemon zest, basil leaves, and freshly ground black pepper, then serve.

**prep + cook time
25 minutes
serves 2–3**

TOFU CHILI
(VEGAN)

10oz (280g) firm tofu, patted
   dry and finely chopped
1 tbsp extra virgin olive oil
1 onion, finely chopped
3 garlic cloves, crushed
1 red bell pepper, roughly chopped
¼ cup (60g) chipotle paste
1 tsp smoked paprika
1 tsp ground cumin
1 tsp ground coriander
1 (15.5oz/400g) can kidney beans,
   drained and rinsed
1 (14.5oz/400g) can diced tomatoes
1¼ cups (300ml) vegetable stock
1 tbsp maple syrup
juice of 1 lime
to serve: handful of roughly chopped
   cilantro

1 Preheat the air fryer to 400°F/200°C for 3 minutes.
2 Put the tofu into a baking dish that fits in the air fryer, then drizzle with the oil. Cook at 400°F/200°C for 10 minutes until browned.
3 Add the onion, garlic, red pepper, chipotle paste, paprika, cumin, and coriander. Mix well, and cook at 350°F/180°C for 10 minutes.
4 Add the kidney beans, diced tomatoes, and vegetable stock. Cook at 350°F/180°C for 20 minutes until the sauce has reduced.
5 Add the maple syrup and lime juice, then season with salt and freshly ground black pepper.

6 To serve, sprinkle with the cilantro.

SERVE IT Serve with basmati rice.

TIP The tofu chili can be made a day in advance.

prep + cook time
45 minutes
serves 4

PESTO ORZO BAKE

1 shallot, finely chopped

1 garlic clove, crushed

1 zucchini, chopped

1 yellow bell pepper, seeded and roughly chopped

1 tbsp extra virgin olive oil

2 tbsp pesto

8oz (225g) orzo

1½ cups (340ml) boiling vegetable stock or water

¾ cup (100g) frozen peas

juice of 1 lemon

3½oz (100g) soft goat cheese

2 tbsp roughly chopped flat-leaf parsley

1 Preheat the air fryer to 300°F/150°C for 3 minutes.
2 To a baking dish that fits in the air fryer, add the shallot, garlic, zucchini, and yellow pepper. Drizzle with the olive oil, and cook at 300°F/150°C for 5 minutes until the vegetables have softened.
3 Preheat the air fryer to 350°F/180°C for 3 minutes. Add in the pesto, orzo, stock or water, and peas. Mix well, then cover tightly with foil, and cook at 350°F/180°C for about 25 minutes until the stock has evaporated and the orzo is tender.
4 Add the lemon juice, and season with salt and black pepper. Dot with the goat cheese, then sprinkle with the parsley and serve.

prep + cook time

35 minutes

serves 2

ROASTED EGGPLANT WITH HARISSA (VEGAN)

2 tbsp harissa paste
1 tsp ras el hanout
¼ cup (60ml) extra virgin olive oil
2 eggplants (1½lb/700g), cut in
   half lengthwise
1 (15oz/425g) can chickpeas,
   drained and rinsed
2 red onions, cut into wedges
5oz (150g) cherry tomatoes
8oz (225g) pearl couscous
2 sprigs of mint, roughly chopped
2 tbsp roughly chopped flat-leaf
   parsley, plus extra to serve
juice of 1 lemon

1 Preheat the air fryer to 350°F/180°C for 3 minutes.
2 In a small bowl, whisk together the harissa paste, ras el hanout, and oil.
3 Place the eggplants cut-side up in the air fryer basket. Brush with half of the harissa oil and cook at 350°F/180°C for 20 minutes.
4 In a medium bowl, combine the chickpeas, onions, and cherry tomatoes. Pour in the remaining harissa oil, and mix well to coat.
5 Turn the eggplants over so they are cut-side down. Add the chickpeas and vegetables to the air fryer with the eggplant.

6 Cook at 350°F/180°C for 15 minutes until the eggplants are soft and the vegetables are tender.
7 Meanwhile, cook the couscous according to package instructions. Once the couscous is ready, add the chopped mint and parsley and the lemon juice, then season with salt and black pepper.
8 Serve the eggplants over the couscous, with some extra parsley on top.

**prep + cook time
40 minutes
serves 2–3**

TANDOORI PANEER

4 tbsp (50g) tandoori paste
2 garlic cloves, crushed
¾-in (2-cm) piece of ginger, peeled and finely grated
⅓ cup (75g) plain yogurt
8oz (225g) paneer, cut into 2½-in (6-cm) squares
1 green bell pepper, seeded and cut into 1¼-in (3-cm) pieces
1 red onion, cut into small wedges
vegetable or olive oil cooking spray
to serve: lemon wedges

TOMATO SALAD:
4 tomatoes, chopped
½ red onion, finely chopped
½ cucumber, seeded and chopped
3 tbsp roughly chopped cilantro
juice of 1 lime

1 Soak eight wooden skewers in water for 10 minutes.
2 In a medium bowl, mix together the tandoori paste, garlic, ginger, and yogurt. Add the paneer, and set aside to marinate for 20 minutes.
3 Preheat the air fryer to 375°F/190°C for 3 minutes.
4 Assemble the skewers, beginning with a piece of paneer, then a piece of pepper, and finishing with the red onion.
5 Put the skewers into the air fryer basket, spray with cooking spray, and cook at 375°F/190°C for 9 minutes until charred.
6 In a medium bowl, make the salad by combining the tomatoes, red onion, cucumber, and cilantro. Squeeze in the lime juice, and season with salt and black pepper.
7 Serve the paneer skewers on a platter, with the salad and lemon wedges on the side.

TIP You can marinate the paneer for up to 24 hours if you have time.

prep + cook time
15 minutes, plus marinating time
serves 2

ASPARAGUS & GRUYÈRE TARTS

¾lb (300g) asparagus, woody ends
   snapped off
1 tbsp extra virgin olive oil
1 sheet premade puff pastry
2 tbsp Dijon mustard
scant ½ cup (50g) finely grated
   Gruyère
scant ¼ cup (15g) finely grated
   Parmesan
2 sprigs of tarragon, leaves picked
1 egg, beaten

1 Preheat the air fryer to 340°F/170°C for 3 minutes.
2 Put the asparagus into a medium bowl, drizzle with the oil, and season with black pepper. Set aside.
3 Unroll the pastry and cut it into four rectangular pieces. Spread the Dijon mustard over each piece, leaving a 1¼-in (3-cm) border at each edge.
4 Sprinkle both cheeses onto the pastries, and top with the asparagus and tarragon.

5 Brush the edges with the beaten egg, then put all the pastries into the air fryer basket.
6 Cook at 340°F/170°C for 15 minutes until puffed up. Season with black pepper and serve.

cook + prep time
18 minutes
serves 4

CAULIFLOWER BAKED RICE

½lb (225g) cauliflower, cut into
  small florets
2 tbsp curry paste
2 garlic cloves, crushed
¾-in (2-cm) piece of ginger, peeled
  and finely grated
1 tsp garam masala
½ tsp chili powder
½ tsp ground turmeric
1 tbsp extra virgin olive oil
1 cup (150g) basmati rice
⅔ cup (150ml) coconut milk
⅔ cup (150ml) boiling water
⅓ cup (50g) raisins
handful of cilantro
⅓ cup (25g) toasted slivered
  almonds
to serve: plain yogurt (optional)

1 Preheat the air fryer to 340°F/170°C for 3 minutes.
2 In a baking dish that fits in the air fryer, combine the cauliflower, curry paste, garlic, ginger, garam masala, chili powder, turmeric, and olive oil, then mix well.
3 Cook at 340°F/170°C for 10 minutes until the cauliflower florets are slightly caramelized.
4 Put the rice into a strainer and rinse well under cold water, then set aside.
5 Add the coconut milk to a small saucepan and bring to a boil.
6 To the baking dish, add the rice, coconut milk, boiling water, and raisins. Season with salt, and tightly seal the dish with foil.

7 Cook at 340°F/170°C for 25 minutes until the liquid has been absorbed and the rice is tender.
8 Top with the cilantro and almonds, and serve with yogurt, if you like.

TIP Swap the yogurt to dairy-free yogurt to make this vegan.

**prep + cook time
40 minutes
serves 2**

TERIYAKI NOODLES

8oz (225g) button mushrooms, sliced into ½-in (1-cm) strips

½ onion, sliced

¾-in (2-cm) piece of ginger, peeled and finely grated

1 tsp minced garlic

½ tsp chili flakes

1 tbsp vegetable oil

3½oz (100g) broccolini, cut in half widthwise

2 eggs, beaten

2 tbsp teriyaki sauce

14oz (410g) fresh egg noodles

2 tbsp roughly chopped cilantro

to serve: lime wedges (optional)

1 Preheat the air fryer to 375°F/190°C for 3 minutes.

2 In a baking dish that fits in the air fryer, combine the mushrooms, onion, ginger, garlic, and chili flakes. Drizzle with the oil, stir, then cook at 375°F/190°C for 5 minutes.

3 Add the broccolini, and cook at 375°F/190°C for a further 5 minutes.

4 Push the vegetables to one side of the dish, and add the beaten eggs into the space. Cook at 375°F/190°C for 3 minutes until the eggs are set.

5 Break the eggs up with a wooden spoon. Add the teriyaki, noodles, and a splash of water. Mix everything together and cook at 375°F/190°C for 2 minutes.

6 Sprinkle with the cilantro and serve with lime wedges, if liked.

TIP Substitute the vegetables for whatever you have in the fridge; peppers, baby corn, and carrots work well.

prep + cook time
25 minutes
serves 2

WEEKEND

Weekends are for enjoying something a little bit more special. Entertain friends with a nut roast or butternut squash wellington. The air fryer is ideal for sides too, whether it's a leek and cannellini bean casserole, or cheesy potatoes au gratin.

RED ONION GALETTE

2 large red onions, thinly sliced
1 tbsp extra virgin olive oil
1 tbsp light brown sugar
1 tbsp balsamic vinegar
1 sheet premade puff pastry
1 egg, beaten
1 cup (100g) grated Gruyère
3 sprigs of thyme, leaves picked
to serve: crème fraîche or sour
    cream and a leafy salad

1 Preheat the air fryer to 325°F/160°C for 3 minutes.
2 Put the onions in a baking dish that fits in the air fryer, then drizzle with the olive oil, and sprinkle with a little salt. Cook at 325°F/160°C for 15–20 minutes.
3 Add the brown sugar and balsamic vinegar. Mix well, and cook at 325°F/160°C for 10 minutes until caramelized and jammy. Set aside to cool.
4 Preheat the air fryer to 340°F/170°C for 3 minutes. Unroll the pastry, and cut out the largest circle possible from the sheet.
5 Fold over 2in (5cm) from the edge of the pastry into the middle of the circle, then brush the edges with the beaten egg.
6 Prick the pastry with a fork, then put into the air fryer basket, and cook at 340°F/170°C for 10 minutes.
7 Sprinkle the cheese over the middle of the galette, and then spread on the onions. Cook at 340°F/170°C for 5 minutes until golden.
8 Sprinkle with the thyme and some black pepper.
9 Serve with crème fraîche and a leafy salad.

prep + cook time
45 minutes
serves 2

HERBY FALAFEL (VEGAN)

1 (15oz/425g) can chickpeas, drained and rinsed
½ cup (20g) roughly chopped flat-leaf parsley
½ cup (20g) roughly chopped cilantro
3 sprigs of mint, roughly chopped
1 garlic clove, crushed
½ red onion, roughly chopped
1 tsp ground cumin
1 tsp za'atar
grated zest of 1 lemon
vegetable or olive oil cooking spray
to serve: toasted pita breads, hummus, shredded romaine lettuce, guindilla peppers, sliced tomato, and sliced cucumber

1 Add the chickpeas, parsley, cilantro, mint, garlic, onion, cumin, za'atar, and lemon zest to a blender. Season with salt and pepper, then pulse until the mixture comes together but still retains some texture.
2 Roll the mixture into 3½-oz (50-g) balls and place on a tray.
3 Preheat the air fryer to 375°F/190°C for 3 minutes.
4 Put the falafels into the air fryer basket, then spray generously with cooking spray. Cook at 375°F/190°C for 15 minutes until cooked through and golden in color.

5 Serve the falafel with the pitas, hummus, lettuce, guindilla peppers, tomato, and cucumber.

**prep + cook time
20 minutes
serves 2**

TOMATO & RICOTTA LASAGNA

---

3 tbsp extra virgin olive oil
½ onion, finely chopped
2 garlic cloves, crushed
1 (14.5oz/400g) can diced tomatoes
3½oz (100g) cherry tomatoes
1 cup (250g) ricotta
grated zest of 1 lemon
5 lasagna noodles
¼ cup (50g) pesto
5½oz (150g) ball mozzarella, thinly sliced
¼ cup (15g) roughly chopped basil

1 Heat the oil in a medium saucepan, then add the onion and garlic. Add a pinch of salt and sauté for 5 minutes until the onion has softened.

2 Add the diced tomatoes and the cherry tomatoes. Cook over medium heat for 15 minutes until the diced tomatoes have reduced and the cherry tomatoes have softened but are still holding their shape. Season with salt and pepper and set aside.

3 Meanwhile, in a small bowl, combine the ricotta and lemon zest. Season with salt and pepper, mix well and set aside.

4 In a shallow baking dish, soak the lasagna noodles in hot water for 5 minutes.

5 Preheat the air fryer to 340°F/170°C for 3 minutes.

6 In a baking dish that fits in the air fryer, start to assemble the lasagna. Begin with a layer of the tomato sauce, then add a lasagna noodle (you may have to cut this down to fit). Spread with some pesto. Dot with the ricotta and mozzarella, then sprinkle with some basil. Repeat until you have five layers, finishing with the cheese on top.

7 Tightly cover with foil and cook at 340°F/170°C for 30 minutes. Remove the foil, and cook uncovered for a further 10 minutes until golden.

TIP This can be assembled the day before cooking.

prep + cook time
1 hour 10 minutes
serves 2

POTATOES AU GRATIN
WITH CHEESE

1¾ cups (400ml) heavy cream
3 garlic cloves, crushed
6 tbsp (80g) butter, melted
1½lb (700g) potatoes, peeled and
   very finely sliced
3 sprigs of thyme, leaves picked
scant 2 cups (225g) grated cheddar
⅓ cup (100ml) vegetable stock

1 Preheat the air fryer to 325°F/160°C for 3 minutes.
2 Add the cream, garlic, and butter to a measuring cup, then mix well.
3 In a baking dish that fits in the air fryer, add a layer of potatoes, then pour over some of the cream mixture. Add a sprinkle of thyme, and sprinkle with cheese. Repeat this layering process five times, reserving some cheese and thyme for the end.
4 Pour in the vegetable stock, cover tightly with foil, and put the dish into the air fryer. Cook at 325°F/160°C for 40 minutes until the potatoes have softened.
5 Remove the foil, sprinkle with the remaining cheese, increase the heat of the air fryer, and cook at 375°F/190°C for 10 minutes until bubbling and golden. Sprinkle with the rest of the thyme to serve.

cook + prep time
55 minutes
serves 4

NUT ROAST
WITH LENTILS & MUSHROOMS (VEGAN)

½oz (15g) porcini mushrooms
1 onion, finely chopped
2 garlic cloves, crushed
1 carrot, finely chopped
1 celery stick, finely chopped
3½oz (100g) button mushrooms, finely chopped
2 sprigs of rosemary, finely chopped
2 tbsp extra virgin olive oil
1 cup (100g) mixed nuts, such as walnuts, hazelnuts, and pistachios, finely chopped
⅛ cup (20g) dried apricots, finely chopped
3 cups (150g) fresh breadcrumbs
1 (9oz/250g) pouch ready-to-eat lentils
⅓ cup (100ml) vegetable stock
2 eggs, beaten

1 Put the porcini mushrooms in a small bowl, then add ⅓ cup (100ml) boiling water and set aside for 15 minutes.
2 Preheat the air fryer to 300°F/150°C for 3 minutes.
3 Add the onion, garlic, carrot, celery, button mushrooms, and rosemary to a 8 x 5in (20 x 13cm) loaf pan. Drizzle with the olive oil and season with salt and black pepper. Cook at 300°F/150°C for 15 minutes until softened and the mushrooms have taken on color. Transfer the mixture to a medium bowl.
4 Drain the porcini mushrooms, keeping the liquid, and finely chop. Add the porcini mushrooms and their liquid to the bowl.

5 Add the nuts, apricots, breadcrumbs, lentils, vegetable stock, and eggs. Season with salt and black pepper and mix well.
6 Preheat the air fryer to 340°F/170°C for 3 minutes. Line the loaf pan with parchment paper. Put the mixture into the pan, then, using the back of a spoon, press it down well. Cook at 340°F/170°C for 30 minutes until dark in color and firm to touch.
7 Let cool for 10 minutes, then remove from the pan and serve.

Prep + cook time
1 hour 10 minutes
serves 4

BAKED POTATOES
WITH CARAMEL- IZED GREEN ONION (VEGAN)

6 green onions
6½ tbsp extra virgin olive oil
1 tbsp capers, roughly chopped
juice of ½ lemon
2 tbsp finely snipped chives
2 tbsp finely chopped dill
2 large Russet potatoes
1 cup (200g) canned lima beans,
   drained and rinsed
to serve: dairy-free yogurt (optional)

1 Preheat the air fryer to 400°F/200°C for 3 minutes.
2 Put the green onions into the air fryer basket, and drizzle with 1 tablespoon olive oil. Cook at 400°F/200°C for 6 minutes until soft and caramelized.
3 Meanwhile, in a small bowl, combine the capers, lemon juice, chives, dill, and 3½ tablespoons olive oil. Set aside.
4 Roughly chop the caramelized green onions. Add them to the dressing, mix again, and set aside.
5 Pierce the potatoes and rub 1 tablespoon olive oil on each one. Sprinkle with salt, and put them into the air fryer.

6 Cook at 400°F/200°C for 40 minutes until the potatoes are golden and crisp on the outside, but soft within.
7 Cut the potatoes open, add the beans, and cook at 400°F/200°C for a further minute to warm the beans through.
8 Serve the baked potatoes with the dressing and a spoonful of dairy-free yogurt, if you like.

prep + cook time
50 minutes
serves 2

127

BEAN BURGERS

1 (15.5oz/400g) can lima beans,
   drained and rinsed
1 zucchini, grated
2¼ cups (100g) panko breadcrumbs
½ red onion, finely chopped
2 garlic cloves, crushed
1 tbsp ground cumin
½ tsp cayenne pepper
1 egg
handful of roughly chopped cilantro
4 burger buns
1 head butter lettuce, leaves
   separated
4 slices of American cheese
½ red onion, sliced
vegetable or olive oil cooking spray
to serve: mayonnaise and ketchup

1 Preheat the air fryer to 350°F/180°C for 3 minutes.
2 In a medium bowl, mash the lima beans with a fork. Add the zucchini, panko, red onion, garlic, cumin, cayenne, egg, and cilantro. Season well with salt and black pepper, and mix.
3 Shape the mixture into four patties.
4 Put the patties into the air fryer basket, spray with cooking spray, then cook at 350°F/180°C for 10 minutes.
5 Turn the patties over, spray with a little more cooking spray, and cook for a further 5 minutes until golden in color.

6 Meanwhile, halve and toast the burger buns.
7 Spread mayonnaise on the base of each burger bun, then add a couple of lettuce leaves. Add a bean burger patty on top, a slice of cheese, and some red onion, and finish with some ketchup on the burger lid.

TIP You can substitute the lima beans with chickpeas or kidney beans, if you like.

**prep + cook time
20 minutes
serves 4**

CAULIFLOWER TACOS

½ red onion, thinly sliced

juice of 2 limes, divided, plus 1 lime cut into wedges

2lb (900g) cauliflower, cut into small florets

1 tbsp fajita seasoning

1 tbsp oregano

1 tbsp extra virgin olive oil

2 ripe avocados, peeled and pitted

¼ cup (50g) Greek yogurt

1 green onion, thinly sliced

1 red chile, seeded and finely chopped

6 flour tortillas

2 radishes, cut into thin matchsticks

3 tbsp cilantro leaves

to serve: hot sauce (optional)

1 In a small bowl, combine the red onion, juice of 1 lime and a pinch of salt. Mix and set aside.

2 Preheat the air fryer to 375°F/190°C for 3 minutes.

3 In a medium bowl, combine the cauliflower, fajita seasoning, oregano, and oil. Season with salt and pepper and add to the air fryer basket.

4 Cook the cauliflower at 375°F/190°C for 15 minutes until lightly caramelized and tender.

5 Meanwhile, in a small bowl, mash the avocados lightly with a fork. Add the yogurt, green onion, red chile, and the juice of 1 lime. Season with salt and black pepper, mix and set aside.

6 Heat the tortillas in a dry, hot pan, then keep warm under a sheet of foil.

7 To assemble the tacos, spoon some of the avocado crème over a tortilla, top with the cauliflower, radishes, pickled onion, and cilantro. Serve with some hot sauce, if liked.

TIP To make these tacos vegan, swap the Greek yogurt with dairy-free yogurt.

prep + cook time
25 minutes
serves 2

MUSHROOM SHAWARMA (VEGAN)

¼ red cabbage, thinly sliced
12oz (325g) portobello mushrooms, cut into ½-in (1-cm) slices
1 red onion, cut into wedges
1 tsp minced garlic
1 tsp ground cumin
1 tsp smoked paprika
1 tsp ground coriander
2 tbsp soy sauce
½ tbsp maple syrup
1 tbsp extra virgin olive oil
2 tbsp tahini
juice of ½ lemon
2 pita breads
to serve: guindilla peppers and flat-leaf parsley

1 Add the cabbage to a medium bowl, sprinkle with a little salt, mix, and set aside.
2 In a medium bowl, combine the sliced mushrooms, red onion wedges, garlic, cumin, paprika, coriander, soy sauce, maple syrup, and olive oil. Season with salt and black pepper, then set aside for 15 minutes to marinate.
3 Preheat the air fryer to 410°F/210°C for 3 minutes.
4 Put a sheet of foil in the air fryer basket, then add the mushrooms and red onion. Cook at 410°F/210°C for 20 minutes until the mushrooms are crispy and the red onion is caramelized and tender.

5 Meanwhile, in a small bowl, combine the tahini, lemon juice and 2 tablespoons water. Whisk until smooth and set aside.
6 Toast the pitas, then cut a pocket in them. Fill them with the tahini sauce, mushrooms, and onions, and add some red cabbage. Serve with a few guindilla peppers and parsley leaves on the side.

**prep + cook time
30 minutes, plus
marinating time
serves 2**

CABBAGE ROLLS (VEGAN)

1 onion, finely chopped
2 garlic cloves, crushed
1 tbsp extra virgin olive oil
8 large Napa cabbage leaves
1 (9oz/250g) pouch ready-to-eat
  lentils
juice of 1 lemon
¼ cup (40g) dried apricots,
  finely chopped
½ cup (20g) finely chopped
  flat-leaf parsley
⅓ cup (15g) finely chopped cilantro
⅓ cup (100ml) tomato sauce
2 tbsp tomato paste
1 tbsp red wine vinegar

1 Preheat the air fryer to 300°F/150°C for 3 minutes. **2** Put the onion and garlic in a baking dish that fits in the air fryer. Drizzle with the olive oil, add a pinch of salt, then cook at 300°F/150°C for 5 minutes. **3** Bring a large pan of water to a boil. Add the cabbage leaves and boil 5 minutes until softened. Drain and rinse with cold water. **4** Put the lentils into a medium bowl, add the onion, garlic, lemon juice, apricots, parsley, and cilantro. Season with salt and black pepper, and mix. **5** Lay the cabbage leaves out flat and remove the stalks. Put a couple tablespoons of the lentil mixture into the center of each leaf. Fold the sides in and roll away from you, leaving no exposed edges. **6** Put the stuffed leaves in a baking dish that fits in the air fryer. Preheat the air fryer to 340°F/170°C for 3 minutes. In a measuring cup, mix the tomato sauce, tomato paste, and red wine vinegar, then pour around the cabbage leaves, and cover tightly with foil. Cook at 340°F/170°C for 30 minutes until softened.

**prep + cook time
40 minutes
serves 2**

BAKED CAMEMBERT
WITH TEAR & SHARE BREAD

1¾ cups (250g) bread flour
1 tsp salt
1 packet (7g) fast-action yeast
1 tsp sugar
2 garlic cloves, crushed
2 tbsp roughly chopped flat-leaf
  parsley
2 tbsp (25g) butter, melted
1 vegetarian Camembert
vegetable or olive oil cooking spray

1 To a large bowl or stand mixer, add the flour, salt, yeast, and sugar. Make a well in the center of the flour, then slowly mix in ⅔ cup (150ml) warm water. Mix until the dough has come together.

2 Turn out onto the counter and knead for 10 minutes. Or, if using a stand mixer, knead for 5 minutes with a dough hook until smooth.

3 Oil a round baking dish that fits in the air fryer. Divide the dough into six equal pieces and roll them into round balls. Arrange them in the dish in a circle, leaving space between them to prove and space in the middle for the Camembert. Cover with a damp kitchen towel and prove for 30 minutes.

4 Preheat the air fryer to 350°F/180°C for 3 minutes.

5 Put the bread into the air fryer and cook at 350°F/180°C for 25 minutes until risen and golden.

6 Add the crushed garlic and chopped parsley to the melted butter.

7 Remove the bread from the air fryer, brush with the garlic butter then set aside.

8 Unwrap the Camembert then place it back in the box. Cut a crosshatch pattern on the top, lower the heat of the air fryer, and cook at 300°F/150°C for 7 minutes until the cheese is gooey.

9 Put the Camembert into the center of the bread rolls and serve.

**prep + cook time
50 minutes, plus proving time
serves 3–4**

SWEET POTATO & BLACK BEAN

ENCHILADAS

- 1 lb (450g) sweet potato, peeled and cut into ¾-in (2-cm) cubes
- 1 red onion, finely chopped
- 1 tsp smoked paprika
- 1 tbsp chipotle paste
- 1 (15oz/425g) can black beans, drained and rinsed
- 1 red chile, seeded and finely chopped
- 2 tbsp roughly chopped cilantro, plus extra to serve
- 1 tbsp extra virgin olive oil
- 6 corn tortillas
- 1¼ cups (300ml) enchilada sauce
- 1½ cups (150g) grated cheddar
- 2 tbsp crispy onions

1 Fill a large saucepan with water and bring to a boil. Once boiling, add the sweet potato and cook for 10 minutes until soft. Drain, add to a medium bowl and mash half of the sweet potato with a fork, leaving half in chunks.
2 To the bowl, add the red onion, paprika, chipotle, black beans, red chile, cilantro, and olive oil. Season with salt and black pepper then set aside.
3 Preheat the air fryer to 350°F/180°C for 3 minutes.
4 Lay the tortillas out flat, and divide the mixture among the tortillas, placing it in the center. Fold the sides into the middle, and roll them up tightly.

5 Put them side by side in a baking dish that fits in the air fryer. Top with the enchilada sauce and cheddar. Cook at 350°F/180°C for 15 minutes. The sauce should be bubbling and the enchiladas should be golden around the edges.
6 Top with the crispy onions and extra cilantro and serve.

SERVE IT Serve with some sour cream and jalapeños on the side, if you like.

prep + cook time
30 minutes
serves 4

LEEK & CANNELLINI BEAN CASSEROLE

2 leeks, trimmed and sliced
2 garlic cloves, thinly sliced
3 sprigs of thyme, leaves picked
2 tbsp extra virgin olive oil
4½ tbsp (70ml) vegetable stock
⅓ cup (100ml) heavy cream
2 tbsp crème fraîche or sour cream
1 tsp Dijon mustard
4 cups (600g) canned cannellini
   beans, drained
2 cups (200g) grated cheddar
1½ cups (80g) fresh breadcrumbs
vegetable or olive oil cooking spray

1 Preheat the air fryer to 325°F/160°C for 3 minutes.
2 In a baking dish that fits in the air fryer, combine the leeks, garlic, and thyme. Drizzle with the olive oil and season with a little salt. Cook at 325°F/160°C for 12 minutes until the leeks have softened.
3 Preheat the air fryer to 340°F/170°C for 3 minutes. Add the vegetable stock, cream, crème fraîche, Dijon mustard, and cannellini beans. Mix well, and cook at 340°F/170°C for 12 minutes until the sauce slightly thickens.
4 Preheat the air fryer to 375°F/190°C for 3 minutes.

Sprinkle with the cheddar and breadcrumbs and spray with cooking spray.
5 Cook at 375°F/190°C for 15 minutes until the sauce is bubbling and the breadcrumbs are golden.

**prep + cook time
45 minutes
serves 3–4**

SPICED LENTIL SHEPHERD'S PIE

1 onion, finely chopped

2 carrots, peeled and finely chopped

2 garlic cloves, crushed

1-in (3-cm) piece ginger, peeled and finely grated

1 tbsp tomato paste

1 tbsp garam masala

1 tbsp curry powder

2 tbsp extra virgin olive oil

1 (9oz/250g) pouch ready-to-eat lentils

⅓ cup (100ml) vegetable stock

1½lb (800g) ready-to-eat mashed potatoes

⅔ cup (80g) grated cheddar

1 Preheat the air fryer to 300°F/150°C for 3 minutes.
2 In a baking dish that fits in the air fryer, combine the onion, carrots, garlic, ginger, tomato paste, garam masala, and curry powder. Drizzle with the olive oil, then sprinkle with a pinch of salt. Cook at 300°F/150°C for 10 minutes until the carrots and onion have softened.
3 Preheat the air fryer to 350°F/180°C for 3 minutes. Add the lentils and vegetable stock, and season with salt and black pepper.
4 Top with the mashed potatoes, then cook at 350°F/180°C for 15 minutes until the potato topping is golden and crispy.
5 Top with the cheese, increase the heat of the air fryer, and cook at 375°F/190°C for 5 minutes until golden.

prep + cook time
40 minutes
serves 4

BUTTERNUT SQUASH WELLINGTON (VEGAN)

---

1 butternut squash, peeled and cut in half lengthwise and widthwise (you only need the top half for this recipe; keep the seeded bottom section for something else)

3 tbsp extra virgin olive oil

1 onion, finely chopped

2 garlic cloves, crushed

2 sprigs of rosemary, finely chopped

11oz (325g) button mushrooms, finely chopped

2½ tbsp pine nuts

14oz (400g) spinach

1 sheet premade vegan puff pastry

2 tbsp plant-based milk

1 Preheat the air fryer to 340°F/170°C for 3 minutes.
2 Put the two butternut squash top halves into the air fryer basket, then drizzle with 1 tablespoon olive oil and season with salt and black pepper. Cook at 340°F/170°C for 20 minutes, then set aside.
3 Into a baking dish that fits in the air fryer, put the onion, garlic, rosemary, mushrooms, and pine nuts. Drizzle with the remaining olive oil, and season with salt and black pepper. Cook at 340°F/170°C for 10 minutes until softened and the mushrooms are golden. Set aside to cool.
4 Put the spinach in a colander in the sink. Pour boiling water over the spinach to wilt, then rinse with cold water from the tap to cool. Squeeze out the excess water and set aside.
5 Unroll the pastry with the shortest side toward you, and cut in half horizontally. On one half of the pastry, begin by laying half of the spinach out flat, then topping with half of the mushroom mixture. Place both halves of the butternut squash on top end to end. Then put the remaining spinach on top of the squash and finish with the remaining mushroom mixture.
6 Place the other half of the pastry on top, crimp the edges with a fork and brush with the milk.
7 Put the wellington into the air fryer basket and cook at 340°F/170°C for 30 minutes until the pastry looks golden and crisp.

prep + cook time
1 hour 10 minutes
serves 4

CAULIFLOWER & CHEESE

2lb (900g) cauliflower, cut into
    florets and leaves reserved
1 tbsp extra virgin olive oil
2 tbsp (20g) butter
2 tbsp all-purpose flour
1¼ cups (300ml) milk
1 tsp spicy mustard
½ tsp cayenne pepper
scant ¼ cup (15g) grated cheddar
3 tbsp (20g) grated mozzarella
2 cups (100g) fresh breadcrumbs
vegetable or olive oil cooking spray

1 Preheat the air fryer to 400°F/200°C for 3 minutes.
2 In a medium bowl, add the cauliflower florets and leaves. Drizzle with the olive oil, season with salt and black pepper, and give it a toss to coat.
3 Put the cauliflower in a baking dish that fits in the air fryer. Cook at 400°F/200°C for 15 minutes until caramelized and softened.
4 Meanwhile, in a medium saucepan, melt the butter. Once foaming, add the flour and mix well for 1 minute. Gradually add the milk, continuing to stir until you have a thick sauce.

5 Add the mustard, cayenne, cheddar, and mozzarella to the sauce. Mix well, then season with salt and black pepper.
6 Pour the sauce onto the cauliflower and top with the breadcrumbs. Spray with cooking spray, lower the heat of the air fryer, and cook at 375°F/190°C for 10 minutes until golden and bubbling.

cook + prep time
35 minutes
serves 2

DESSERTS

The air fryer not only allows you to bake crispy, pastry-topped pies and chewy cookies, it also enables you to make decadent, gooey desserts, such as a self-saucing chocolate cake, which is certain to be a real crowd pleaser.

ROASTED PINEAPPLE
WITH LIME (VEGAN)

1 tbsp maple syrup
1 tsp ground ginger
grated zest and juice of 1 lime
1 pineapple, peeled, cored, and cut
    into wedges
1 tsp turbinado sugar
to serve: coconut yogurt

1 Preheat the air fryer to 410°F/210°C for 3 minutes.
2 In a small bowl, combine the maple syrup, ginger, and lime juice. Brush the mixture onto the pineapple and sprinkle with the turbinado sugar.
3 Line the air fryer basket with foil, add the pineapple, and cook at 410°F/210°C for 15 minutes until caramelized and softened. Sprinkle with the lime zest and serve with coconut yogurt on the side.

prep + cook time
20 minutes
serves 3–4

WHITE CHOCOLATE & GINGER COOKIES

6tbsp (80g) unsalted butter
⅔ cup (130g) light brown sugar
1 egg
1¼ cups (155g) all-purpose flour
1 tsp baking powder
½tsp salt
1 tsp ground ginger
1oz (25g) crystallized ginger,
    roughly chopped
3oz (80g) white chocolate,
    roughly chopped

1 In a small saucepan, melt the butter over medium heat until browned and smelling nutty. Let cool.
2 Add the cooled butter to a medium bowl with the brown sugar, and beat with an electric mixer until pale. Add the egg and beat again until combined.
3 Sift the flour, baking powder, salt, and ground ginger into the bowl, then fold until combined. Stir in the crystallized ginger and white chocolate.
4 Roll the dough into 2 tbsp balls, put on a tray, and place in the fridge for 15 minutes to firm up.
5 Preheat the air fryer to 340°F/170°C for 3 minutes.
6 Line the air fryer basket with parchment paper, and add the cookies, keeping them spaced 2 inches apart. Cook at 340°F/170°C for 15 minutes.
7 As soon as they come out, gently press them with the back of a spoon. Let cool, then serve.

KEEP IT Once rolled into balls, the dough can be stored in the freezer. Freeze them uncovered on a baking sheet, and when frozen, transfer to a freezer bag and store for up to 2 months. To cook from frozen, add 2 minutes to the cooking time.

**prep + cook time
25 minutes, plus chilling time
makes 8**

STRAWBERRY COBBLER

1¾lb (800g) strawberries, hulled, small ones left whole and large ones cut in half

⅔ cup (120g) sugar, divided

1 tbsp cornstarch

juice of ½ lemon

4 sprigs of thyme, leaves picked

1¼ cup (150g) all-purpose flour

1 tsp baking powder

6 tbsp (80g) cold butter, cubed

1 egg

2 tbsp milk

1 Preheat the air fryer to 325°F/160°C for 3 minutes.
2 In a medium bowl, combine the strawberries with ⅓ cup (70g) sugar, the cornstarch, lemon juice, and thyme, then mix well. Put into a baking dish that fits in the air fryer and cook at 325°F/160°C for 10 minutes until the strawberries are jammy but still holding their shape.
3 Meanwhile, in a medium bowl, combine the flour, baking powder, butter, and remaining sugar. Rub the butter in with your fingertips until you have a breadcrumb-like texture.

4 Add the egg and milk, and stir well. Spoon on top of the strawberries, and cook at 325°F/160°C for 20 minutes until the topping is golden and cooked through.

SERVE IT Serve with vanilla ice cream or whipped cream.

**prep + cook time
35 minutes
serves 4**

CHERRY HAND PIES (VEGAN)

1 lb (450g) frozen cherries, defrosted
½ cup (100g) light brown sugar
2 tbsp cornstarch
1 tsp almond extract
juice of 1 orange
1 sheet vegan puff pastry
2 tbsp plant-based milk

1 Preheat the air fryer to 340°F/170°C for 3 minutes.
2 In a baking dish that fits in the air fryer, combine the cherries, brown sugar, cornstarch, almond extract, and orange juice, mixing well. Put into the air fryer and cook at 340°F/170°C for 10 minutes until the cherries are jammy but hold their shape, and the sauce is thick and syrupy.
3 Unroll the pastry and cut into four rectangular pieces. Divide the mixture between two of the pastry rectangles, leaving a 1¼-in (3-cm) border on all edges.

4 Brush the borders with a little of the milk, top with the other pastry rectangles, and lightly crimp the edges with a fork. With a sharp knife, make two slits on the top of each pie. Brush the pastries all over with milk.
5 Cook at 340°F/170°C for 20 minutes until golden.

prep + cook time
35 minutes
serves 2

APPLE & BLUEBERRY PIE

5 cups (600g) blueberries
3 Granny Smith apples, peeled,
    cored, and cut into 1¼-in (3-cm)
    pieces
grated zest and juice of 1 lemon
½ cup (100g) sugar
1 tbsp cornstarch
1 tsp vanilla extract
1 sheet premade pie crust, cut into
    1¼-in (3-cm) strips
1 egg, beaten
1 tbsp turbinado sugar
to serve: ice cream

1 Preheat the air fryer to 340°F/170°C for 3 minutes.
2 In a baking dish that fits in the air fryer, combine the blueberries, apples, lemon zest and juice, sugar, cornstarch, and vanilla extract. Mix well.
3 Using the pie crust, create a lattice pattern on the top of the baking dish. Brush with beaten egg and sprinkle with the turbinado sugar.
4 Cook at 340°F/170°C for 25 minutes until the pastry is golden and the sauce is bubbling.
5 Serve with ice cream.

prep + cook time
30 minutes
serves 4

SELF-SAUCING CHOCOLATE CAKE

1 cup (130g) all-purpose flour
1 tsp baking soda
½ tsp salt
⅓ cup (70g) sugar
3 tbsp unsweetened cocoa powder
3 tbsp (45g) unsalted butter, melted
2 eggs
⅓ cup (90ml) milk
1½ oz (40g) dark chocolate, cut into
  small chunks

SAUCE:
½ cup (120ml) boiling water
2¼ tbsp unsweetened cocoa powder
6 tbsp (80g) dark brown sugar

1 Preheat the air fryer to 285°F/140°C for 3 minutes.
2 To a medium bowl, add the flour, sugar, cocoa powder, butter, eggs, milk, and dark chocolate. Stir until combined, then pour into a baking dish that fits in the air fryer.
3 For the sauce, in a measuring cup, combine the boiling water with the cocoa powder and brown sugar. Mix well and pour the mixture on top of the batter in the baking dish. Do not stir.
4 Put the dish into the air fryer and cook at 285°F/140°C for 30 minutes until set and saucy.

prep + cook time
35 minutes
serves 4

BREAD & BUTTER PUDDING

2 tbsp unsalted butter, softened, for greasing
1 loaf of brioche, cut into thick slices, and then each slice into triangles
2 cups (500ml) vanilla pudding
1 tsp ground cinnamon
2½ tbsp (20g) raisins

1 Preheat the air fryer to 325°F/160°C for 3 minutes.
2 Butter a baking dish that fits in the air fryer. Arrange the brioche in the dish, overlapping the slices. Pour in the pudding, sprinkle with the cinnamon, and leave to soak for 15 minutes.
3 Top with the raisins, cover with foil, and cook at 325°F/160°C for 15 minutes.

4 Take the foil off and cook for another 15 minutes until golden.

**prep + cook time
35 minutes, plus soaking time
serves 4**

BAKLAVA BITES

6 tbsp (80g) unsalted butter
2 tbsp light brown sugar
1 tsp ground cinnamon
⅔ cup (100g) pistachios, finely chopped, plus extra to serve
⅔ cup (100g) walnut halves, finely chopped
4 sheets of phyllo pastry
2 tbsp vegetable oil

SYRUP:
1 cup (200g) sugar
4 tsp honey

1 In a small saucepan, melt the butter, brown sugar, and cinnamon over gentle heat. Add the pistachios and walnuts, stir in, then set aside to cool.
2 Lay one piece of phyllo pastry on the counter, and brush it with vegetable oil. Layer another piece of pastry on top, and brush with more vegetable oil. Repeat this with all four sheets of phyllo. With the longest strip of layered pastry facing you, cut it vertically into four strips.
3 Divide the nut mixture equally among the four strips, placing the mixture at the bottom of the strips.
4 Fold the sides inward, then fold upward from the bottom until you reach the top. Repeat with all four pastries, then place in a baking pan that fits in the air fryer.

5 Brush the pastry with a little more oil and set aside.
6 For the sauce, in a small saucepan, heat the sugar, honey, and scant 1 cup (200ml) water over low heat to dissolve the sugar. Once dissolved, increase the heat and let it reduce for about 20 minutes until syrupy, then set aside.
7 Preheat the air fryer to 325°F/160°C for 3 minutes.
8 Put the baklava into the air fryer and cook at 325°F/160°C for 20 minutes until golden.
9 Pour on the syrup. Sprinkle with some extra pistachios and let cool. Cut each piece in half to serve.

TIP Store in an airtight container for up to a week.

**prep + cook time
55 minutes
serves 6–8**

LEMON DRIZZLE CAKE

---

scant ¾ cup (140g) sugar
½ cup (125g) unsalted butter
2 eggs
1 cup (120g) all-purpose flour
1 tsp baking powder
½ tsp salt
grated zest and juice of 2 lemons, divided
1½ cups (150g) powdered sugar

1 Preheat the air fryer to 325°F/160°C for 3 minutes.
2 Line a round 6-in (15-cm) cake pan that fits in the air fryer with parchment paper.
3 Add the sugar and butter to a medium bowl, and beat with an electric mixer until pale and fluffy. Add the eggs, one by one, and beat again until combined. Add the flour, baking powder, salt, and the zest from 1 lemon and fold until incorporated.
4 Put the batter into the pan and spread it out evenly. Put into the air fryer and cook at 325°F/160°C for 30 minutes until golden and a skewer comes out clean.
5 Meanwhile, in a small bowl, combine the powdered sugar and the lemon juice, mixing well. Set aside.
6 Once the cake is ready, let it cool slightly in the pan, then turn out and let cool completely.
7 Once cool, top with the lemon icing and decorate with the zest of 1 lemon.

TIP Store in an airtight container for 3 days.

prep + cook time
50 minutes
serves 4

CHERRY ALMOND TART

1 sheet premade pie crust
6 tbsp (80g) unsalted
  butter, softened
6½ tbsp (80g) sugar
1 tsp almond extract
2 eggs
¼ cup (35g) all-purpose flour
¼ tsp baking powder
¼ tsp salt
⅔ cup (70g) ground almonds
⅓ cup (80g) cherry preserves
½ cup (100g) frozen cherries,
  defrosted and liquid drained
¼ cup (20g) slivered almonds

1 Preheat the air fryer to 325°F/160°C for 3 minutes.
2 Cut the pastry so it lines the bottom of a 7-in (18-cm) round pan and prick it with a fork. Put a piece of parchment over the pastry, and fill with some baking beans. Put into the air fryer and cook at 325°F/160°C for 15 minutes.
3 Remove the baking beans and parchment and cook at 325°F/160°C for a further 10 minutes.
4 Meanwhile, add the butter and sugar to a medium bowl, and beat with an electric mixer until pale and fluffy. Add the almond extract and eggs, and beat until combined.

Fold in the flour, baking powder, salt, and ground almonds. Set aside.
5 Spread the preserves onto the crust and sprinkle with the cherries. Add the batter to the pan and sprinkle with the almonds.
6 Cook at 325°F/160°C for 25 minutes until a skewer comes out clean.

prep + cook time
55 minutes
serves 4

EARL GREY COOKIES

7 tbsp (100g) unsalted
  butter, softened
½ cup (100g) sugar
1 egg
1½ cups (200g) all-purpose flour,
  plus extra for dusting
grated zest of 2 lemons, divided
tea leaves from 3 Earl Grey tea bags
½ cup (50g) powdered sugar

1 Preheat the air fryer to 325°F/160°C for 3 minutes.
2 In a medium bowl, beat the butter and sugar using an electric mixer until pale and fluffy. Add the egg and beat again until incorporated. Add the flour, zest from 1 lemon, the tea, and a pinch of salt. Bring together with your hands being careful not to overwork the dough.
3 Roll out, using a little flour to help you. Cut out 20 rounds using a 3-in (8-cm) cutter.
4 Line the air fryer basket with parchment paper, and cook at 325°F/160°C for 10 minutes. Remove and let cool.
5 Mix the powdered sugar with 2 tablespoons water until you have a thick icing. Drizzle the icing onto the cookies with a spoon, and sprinkle with the remaining lemon zest to finish.

**prep + cook time
20 minutes
makes 20**